To Love Thee More Dearly

To Love Thee More Dearly

by

Richard J. Huelsman, SJ

Saint Mary's Press
Christian Brothers Publications
Winona, Minnesota

Genuine recycled paper with 10% post-consumer waste.
Printed with soy-based ink.

The publishing team included Carl Koch, development editor; Laurie A. Berg, copy editor; Alan S. Hanson, production editor and typesetter; Maurine R. Twait, art director; Vicki Shuck, illustrator; pre-press, printing, and binding by the graphics division of Saint Mary's Press.

The acknowledgments continue on page 109.

Printed in the United States of America

Printing: 9 8 7 6 5 4 3 2 1

Year: 2005 04 03 02 01 00 99 98 97

ISBN 0-88489-498-3, paper
ISBN 0-88489-507-6, spiral

Contents

Preface

The thirty reflections in this book can help you appreciate the person of Jesus (part 1), appreciate the ways you relate to him and to others (part 2), and stimulate a desire to follow Jesus in your personal life and in the ways you try to direct the currents of society (part 3). The reflections should be especially helpful for persons who, though busy, want more spiritual depth in their life. However, this book invites all kinds of creative uses. So let your imagination run as you take a look at how it can best serve you and your community.

The format of each reflection will suit many different kinds of people, from those who want to read a meditation quickly in the morning and mull it over during the day, to those who want to discuss its content in a small faith community or a group as a follow-up to Renew or a similar program.

The book is divided into three parts, each offering ten reflections. Each reflection is arranged in the same way: a reminder of God's presence, a focusing statement, a Scripture passage for reflection, a brief comment, openings for prayer, questions for group reflection and sharing, a closing reflection, and a concluding prayer or prayer help. The group discussion questions may also easily be used for personal prayer.

When using this book for communal reflection, some groups might want to start discussion immediately after reflecting on the Scripture passage. Others might first want to read through the openings for prayer to warm their heart and ready their mind for discussion. Some might want to use one meditation per meeting, others might prefer more.

Do not feel limited to the ideas in the meditations. Feel free to follow ideas, memories, feelings, impulses to act, or related topics that seem appropriate at the moment. The meditations' titles and the Scripture passages are the real starting points. From there, let the Spirit lead.

Suggestions for Short Periods of Prayer

If you have only a brief time for prayer, read the Scripture passage slowly and grow quiet. Let the text and the Spirit move within you and suggest the first reactions to pray over. Then invite your reactions, express your feelings, have a short heart-to-heart conversation with Jesus.

If you need something more than the Scripture passage to inspire your reflection, read the suggestions in the Openings for Prayer section and those in the Group Reflection and Sharing section until you find something to ponder.

Suggestions for Longer Periods of Prayer

If you have a longer time to pray, the following ideas may help you enter into the richness of prayer:

Begin by relaxing. Become at ease by first recalling that God is near and that God is interested in you and what you are about to do.

Ask God for some grace or insight from this prayer period. Your request might be for a sense of closeness, or for God's help to be more like Jesus according to what the meditation theme suggests.

Immerse yourself in the Scriptures. Read the Scripture passage and commentary very slowly. After reading, pause to listen in wordless quiet for a while to see what reactions you may be having. Any thoughts, imaginings, memories, feelings, or impulses to act? Let these be your basis for prayer. Pause over any of these because the Spirit may be speaking through them. Do not hurry to move on. Linger over them until you are no longer moved by them. Then go on, but do not hesitate to go back and repeat praying over that fruitful area in your next prayer time, particularly if it brought you peace or if it disturbed or repelled you and so ought to be worked through.

Make use of your senses. Another way of immersing yourself in the Scriptures employs the senses and the imagination. Some suggestions follow for using your senses as you listen to the word of God:
• What do you *see* in your imagination? Be very detailed as to people's appearance, Jesus' appearance, the countryside, people's actions, clothing, and facial expressions. What do you make of these?

- What do you *hear?* How are people talking? Who is saying what? in what tone of voice? to whom? What is really going on beneath the dialog?
- What *sensations* of heat or cold, wind, weather, crowdedness do you note? What significance do they have?
- Take the part of one of the persons in the scene. Who are you? What are you seeing, hearing, thinking, and feeling as this person? Or, be in the crowd more passively as a bystander, or as a news reporter or analyst. What report will you send? What are your impressions to be broadcast tonight over a major network?

Use a threefold meditative reading. A threefold process can be used nicely, too. Read the scriptual passage three times—each time slowly, savoring every word and phrase.
- After the first reading, ask, What was said or done?
- After the second, ask, What does this mean?
- After the third, pause to pray for gratitude, joy, sorrow, wonder, or possibly unease. Let such feelings or any interior movement draw you into conversation or to just being wordless with Jesus, which is also good prayer.

Ponder these questions. Ask questions such as Who? What? Where? Why? When? How? For whom? Does it make any difference? Here are some other questions to prompt reflection:
- What is lovable here? And who is lovable?
- How can I help others live this way?
- What in my history bears on this story?
- Is there something here to help me grow toward Jesus or toward my human best?
- Is there challenge here? comfort?
- Does the scriptural passage apply to our time? to social issues?

Simply attend quietly. Quietly, wordlessly stand, sit, or just be near the scene depicted in the passage and watch. Let it work on you as it will.

Conclude. End with a short colloquy, a heart-to-heart conversation. Not every reflection needs to have a definite resolution. At times, however, this will be appropriate. Let the Spirit lead.

It would also be useful to experiment with some of the preceding methods from time to time. Notice which of the suggestions seem to work best for you personally.

Each of the thirty reflections can draw you closer to Jesus, who is the Way, the Truth, and the Life. Use them as you or your group are able to, knowing that simply reminding yourself of Jesus' constant, loving presence can fill you with light. Immersing yourself in each part of the reflection helps you to converse more deeply with the Source of all life. Trust in Jesus to accept the invitation to instruct, inspire, and enfold you.

Part 1:

What Is Jesus Like?

Introduction

What is Jesus like? To find out, imagine that he invites you to be his companion, to walk with him for a while back in Palestine. What impressions might you get? That is what this part is about: ten sketches of Jesus' most striking characteristics drawn from the Gospel of Luke, an Apostle who understood and wrote of Jesus so well.

For group meetings, read silently one or more of the meditations. Then begin discussion as you choose. Other uses might be suggested by your group and by your local circumstances. Notice also how the short prayer helps that follow some of the reflections can provide opportunities for further prayer and discussion if desired.

For private prayer, if pressed for time, you could "read, run, and mull over" the points during the day. If you have more time, you could read slowly and thoughtfully. Then linger wherever you find something to ponder or to talk about with God. Do not feel you must finish the rest of the material if you find depth and satisfaction in just one point. For good prayer, quality is everything. Quantity of material or number of ideas covered is not important.

Feel free to use the questions in the Group Reflection and Sharing section and in the Openings for Prayer section selectively and in whatever way you find useful. They are there simply to trigger your own concerns and thoughts about the meditation topic.

Reflection 1

Jesus, Contemplative-in-Action

Presence. Relax, and recall God's loving presence and interest in your prayer.

Focus. Remember a time within the last week when you felt really focused and fully present to what you were doing. Was there also a time when you were anxious, "spinning your wheels," and your mind was miles from what you were doing?

Jesus, Contemplative-in-Action

Jesus increased in wisdom and in years, and in divine and human favor. (Luke 2:52)

Comment

Most people go unnoticed in the public eye. They have their joys. They have their struggles. But they usually make it through somehow, even with recessions, pressures at work, and strains in marital and family life. So it was with Jesus. To the eye he was simply one of the village youth, learning about family life, tracking foxes, racing with friends, and sharing play and worship with adults and other youth as he grew. But in unseen ways, Jesus was learning things of even greater importance. He was learning to live in God's presence as well as to get work done, and to love God in everyday activity as well as at prayer. He was becoming aware of God's beauty in the Palestinian landscape, and of God's wisdom in Mary's rising oven-loaves. He was beginning to dream about what to do with his life, and to make the Scriptures' prayer his heartfelt prayer, not just a mouthing of words. Without anyone noticing, God was becoming more and more a part of Jesus' everyday life. God was present with a certain fullness to all that he was doing.

Openings for Prayer

What is your inner life like?

What do you think Jesus' thoughts and feelings might have been on a typical day as a young person growing up in Nazareth?

Could your life be more interesting and exciting if you were more aware of life's many possibilities for love of God and neighbor all through the day? if you were attending more fully to what you were doing?

Group Reflection and Sharing

What does the Scripture passage suggest about Jesus?

What is your experience of trying to progress in "wisdom and in years, and in divine and human favor" before God, that is, of trying to live closer to God and Jesus on an ordinary day? What helps you?

We know that God is calling all of us to become more aware of God in everyday life. Do you see some ways that parishes can help? What about getting help from books or articles?

Besides doing good works in one's free time, how can the heart and mind of a person be turned to God while doing office work, factory work, housework, or any other kind of work?

Does this meditation suggest an idea for action, that is, for finding God while on the run?

Closing. Look around you wherever you are. Pick up some ordinary object that you use frequently: a cup, a telephone, a credit card, or a driver's license. Hold it in your hands as you pray.

Offer any intentions that come from your heart.

Prayer. God of the ordinary, thank you for living among us and for sharing all the details of human life in Jesus. May we learn from him to attend to your presence in all that we do. This we ask in his name. Amen.

Reflection 2

Jesus, Everyone's Friend

Presence. Recall God's presence. Relax in God's love.

Focus. Ponder these incomplete statements: I relate easily and comfortably with people who . . . ; I feel less at ease with people who . . .

Jesus, Everyone's Friend

> The tax collectors and sinners were coming near to listen to [Jesus]. And the Pharisees and the scribes were grumbling and saying, "This fellow welcomes sinners and eats with them." (Luke 15:1–2)

Comment

Nothing beats getting along well with people! For this Jesus had a secret. He had an indiscriminate and accepting love of everyone. Many things about a person—qualities our society prizes like handsome appearance, winning personality, adulation of others, or influence—did not seem to matter to Jesus. For him, a person was a person. Period!

Further, Jesus seems to have liked people as well as loved them. We cannot be certain that he spontaneously liked everyone, but at least he treated the unlikable of society with grace.

Openings for Prayer

Are you experiencing the sheer inner pleasure that comes from reaching out in accepting love to other people? If you are not satisfied with how you are doing, try to imagine what your day would be like if you did reach out to others.

What can help us to like people, as well as to love them?

Talk with Jesus about his experience and your experience of relating patiently, caringly, tolerantly to all people.

Some people rejected Jesus. Has this been part of your experience too?

Group Reflection and Sharing

What does the Scripture passage suggest about Jesus?

It would be wonderful if we could like everyone. Can anything help us move closer to this ideal?

What is the quality of hospitality in your home, among your friends, in your parish? Does everyone feel welcome? Do you look askance at anyone?

What makes for a friendly, hospitable atmosphere at work?

What is your experience with making and keeping friends? What helps or hinders your efforts?

If people act cool and unfriendly, what is to be done in light of this passage?

If certain mannerisms of other people annoy you, what is to be done in light of this passage?

What one specific action could be taken in light of this Scripture passage about Jesus?

Closing. Imagine an individual who stretches you toward the edge of your comfort zone. Keep that image before you as you pray.

Offer any intentions that are in your heart.

Prayer. God, universal lover of humankind, you exclude no one from your compassion, kindness, and care. Teach us to welcome others as you welcome us. May our acceptance of all people be sign and sacrament, healing love in a world of broken relationships and social walls. This we ask in Jesus' name. Amen.

Prayer help. If time to pray is hard to find, read a meditation early in the morning and then mull it over during the day.

Reflection 3

Jesus, Humble

Presence. Recall that God is near and is interested in what you are about to do.

Focus. Skim a newspaper or reflect on a newscast, looking for ways that people (individuals, groups, nations) strive for places of honor.

Jesus, Humble

When [Jesus] noticed how the guests chose the places of honor, he told them a parable. "When you are invited by someone to a wedding banquet, do not sit down at the place of honor, in case someone more distinguished than you has been invited by your host; and the host who invited both of you may come and say to you, 'Give this person your place,' and then in disgrace you would start to take the lowest place. But when you are invited, go and sit down at the lowest place, so that when your host comes, he may say to you, 'Friend, move up higher'; then you will be honored in the presence of all who sit at the table with you. For all who exalt themselves will be humbled, and those who humble themselves will be exalted." (Luke 14:7–11)

Comment

Human nature is peculiar. Its strongest drives can get us into the most trouble. For example, everyone likes praise; yet people who are forever seeking it are annoying. People who are modest about their accomplishments endear themselves to us.

The word *humility* comes from Latin words for "earth" and "on the ground." Humility really means accepting the truth about who we are, recognizing both our earthly limitations and our divine giftedness. Like all humble people, Jesus realized that he was completely dependent on the grace of God, who nurtures, gifts, and loves us. All human beings are of equal worth in God's view.

Openings for Prayer

What is your image of yourself at your best? Talk with Jesus about this.

How do you think Jesus saw himself at his best? He was such a blend of qualities!

Are you developing an admiration for Jesus? Why not tell him so, or ask that you may? What quality about him seems to attract you the most?

Compose a litany of thanksgiving for all the reminders in your life that tell you that you are not God but a fallible, needy human being who is nurtured and protected by God, who loves you.

Group Reflection and Sharing

What does the Scripture passage suggest about Jesus?

Nations, teams, businesses, and persons seem preoccupied with being number one. Is a gentler, humbler, and more easygoing approach to life really possible? What might be its advantages? disadvantages?

What does being humble mean in deed?

What is your experience with trying to be humble?

Can a humble person get ahead? To a humble person, does it matter?

Jesus seemed not only assertive but even aggressive when driving the money changers from the Temple. Yet he was also humble; he said, "'Learn from me; for I am gentle and humble in heart'" (Matthew 11:29).

What might we learn from Jesus' humility?

Can one be too humble?

Does this meditation suggest any idea for action?

Closing. Reflect on a quality in yourself that others find attractive. Rest quietly in appreciation of that gift. Thank God, who gave you the gift.

Offer any intentions that come from your heart.

Prayer. Repeat slowly and silently, in union with your breath: "Jesus meek and humble of heart, make our heart like unto yours." Let each line flow with a breath, in and out. Or make up your own use for this prayer time.

Prayer help. Read the Scripture text slowly. Pause wherever and whenever you find something of interest to reflect on or talk with Jesus about. If you want added stimulation, ask what the passage might mean to you, to others, or to the world, and why Jesus did what he did or said what he said.

Reflection 4

Jesus, Courageous About Money

Presence. Recall how near God is and how special you are to your Creator.

Focus. How satisfied are you with your current financial situation? What would you do with more money if you had it?

Jesus, Courageous About Money

A certain ruler asked [Jesus], "Good Teacher, what must I do to inherit eternal life?" Jesus said to [the ruler], "Why do you call me good? No one is good but God alone. You know the commandments: 'You shall not commit adultery; You shall not murder; You shall not steal; You shall not bear false witness; Honor your father and mother.'" He replied, "I have kept all these since my youth." When Jesus heard this, he said to [the ruler], "There is still one thing lacking. Sell all that you own and distribute the money to the poor, and you will have treasure in heaven; then come, follow me." But when [the ruler] heard this, he became sad; for he was very rich. (Luke 18:18–23)

Comment

Jesus had the courage to say that being poor in spirit and sharing with poor people was necessary, and that actually being poor had advantages. Like most of us, his listeners realized that it was nice to have money. As someone said: "It isn't that I care about money. It's just that having a bundle quiets my nerves!" However, God arranged Jesus' lifestyle to be simple. He had nowhere to lay his head, after all. Why, do you suppose?

Openings for Prayer

The pressures of modern living and the example of peers keep calling for *more*. So how are we to live like Christ's people in an affluent society? What example will we leave for the next generation?

Consider the history of how you use and spend money. If considering the topic is challenging and troublesome, take up these difficulties with Jesus. See what you can work out together.

Group Reflection and Sharing

What does the Scripture passage suggest about Jesus?

Jesus' sayings about riches are some of the most difficult to hear in the entire Gospel. What good do you think he had in mind for us by offering this challenge?

John Wesley is said to have remarked:

> Make all the money you can.
> Save all the money you can.
> Give all the money you can.

What do you think of this advice?

What message does this Scripture passage have for poor people?

What do the salaries paid to professional athletes, actresses and actors, and many CEOs say to teachers, electricians, assembly line workers, nurses, or those involved in ministry? What would Jesus say about this situation?

Can you think of role models when it comes to a Christian use of money?

What are the best and worst causes to give donations to? Why?

Closing. Choose one practical way to live out the fruits of this reflection.

Offer any intentions that you have in your heart.

Prayer. Generous God, giver of all gifts, may we fix our gaze on you, our beginning and our end. Grant us wisdom to use rightly all that we have received, for the good of all. We ask this in Jesus' name. Amen.

Prayer help. After reading the Scripture passage, and also after talking with Jesus at any time, grow quiet and wait for a response. A "response" means a thought, feeling, memory, image, or impulse of the heart to act. A clear response will not always come, but sometimes it will. When it does, make it material for a prayer conversation with Jesus then and there.

Reflection 5

Jesus, Fierce Against Evil

Presence. Recall that the loving God dwells in and around us.

Focus. Of all the stories about evil that you have heard lately, which one or ones touch you the most?

Jesus, Fierce Against Evil

"You Pharisees clean the outside of the cup and of the dish, but inside you are full of greed and wickedness. . . .

"But woe to you Pharisees! For you tithe . . . and neglect justice and the love of God. . . . You love to have the seat of honor in the synagogues and to be greeted with respect in the marketplaces. . . .

"Woe also to you lawyers! For you load people with burdens hard to bear, and you yourselves do not lift a finger to ease them." (Luke 11:39–46)

"You blind guides! You strain out a gnat but swallow a camel!

" . . . You are like whitewashed tombs, which on the outside look beautiful, but inside they are full of the bones of the dead and of all kinds of filth.

"You brood of vipers! How can you escape being sentenced to hell?" (Matthew 23:24–27,33)

Comment

We usually think of pain and suffering as enemies to our happiness. But for Jesus, evildoing and sin were even worse. He confronted them at every turn and told his disciples to do the same—unapologetically and vigorously!

Openings for Prayer

Jesus uses strong language. What do you make of these passages?

As to fighting evil, do you feel called to make any changes in what you are doing at present?

If there are millions of good Christians in this country, how can there be so much crime and so many problems?

In making things better, where does one start?

Group Reflection and Sharing

What does the Scripture passage suggest about Jesus?

What images and words do you associate with evil? How do you feel about the word *evil?*

As you look about the world, life seems such a battle between good and evil. Does either side seem to be winning?

How has evil touched you?

If Jesus was interviewed on a talk show today about the evils of our time, what do you think he would say? What reactions might he receive, and how might he respond?

Do you think Jesus would have lived longer and accomplished more if he had been less confrontational? Would a Dale Carnegie course on *How to Win Friends and Influence People* have helped?

In fighting evil, how does one maintain a certain cheerfulness, courage, hope, and a willingness to keep on fighting even if results are sparse?

In your local community or work situation, is there some evil that ought to be addressed?

"Oh, what can anyone do, it's almost useless to try?" Does this meditation suggest any idea for practical action?

Closing. Share with God your great desire for goodness and justice in our world.

Offer any intentions that are in your heart.

Prayer

Happy those who fear Yahweh,
and joyfully keep God's commandments!

.   .   .   .

Even in the darkness, light dawns for the upright,
for the merciful, compassionate, and righteous.
These good of heart lend graciously,
handling their affairs honestly.
Kept safe by virtue, they are always steadfast
and leave an everlasting memory behind them.

(Psalm 112:1–6)

Prayer help. Talk with Jesus, not only about your thoughts but about your feelings—all of them, positive and negative. Be real with Jesus.

Reflection 6

Jesus, Healer

Presence. Prepare to enter into prayer by recalling God's healing presence.

Focus. What are some ways that people today need healing? Include yourself in "the people."

Jesus, Healer

> Soon afterwards [Jesus] went to a town called Nain, and his disciples and a large crowd went with him. As he approached the gate of the town, a man who had died was being carried out. He was his mother's only son, and she was a widow; and with her was a large crowd from the town. . . . [Jesus] had compassion for her and said to her, "Do not weep." Then he came forward and touched the bier, and the bearers stood still. And he said, "Young man, I say to you, rise!" The dead man sat up and began to speak, and Jesus gave him to his mother. (Luke 7:11–15)

Comment

One gets the impression from the Gospel that Jesus got up in the morning feeling that somehow he was going to heal or leave better whomever he touched that day. He seems almost eager to get on with the preaching, healing, and confronting of evil that made up his days. It was as if he got up saying, "Today is going to be a good day." And it is. It is!

Openings for Prayer

Do you ever think of yourself as being a pleasant and healing kind of person? Have you ever helped heal a relationship, a friend or loved one who was ill, a painful situation? If seeing yourself as a healer is hard to imagine, talk with Jesus about it.

Take a moment to consider something that you might want healing for, and pray earnestly that it may happen.

Group Reflection and Sharing

What does the Scripture passage suggest about Jesus?

Have you had a special experience of healing or being healed? Recall and relate this experience.

Imagine what it would be like if a nation chose to be a healing presence in the world. What might people accomplish?

Can you also envision your community, parish, or congregation as a healing presence in your town or neighborhood? What wounds need attention?

How can you contribute to the healing of family life?

Closing. Can you reach out and touch someone with healing love this week? If so, when will you do it?
Offer any intentions that come from your heart.

Prayer

Loving God, make me an instrument of your peace.
Where there is hatred, let me sow love;
where there is injury, pardon;
where there is discord, union;
where there is doubt, faith;
where there is despair, hope;
where there is darkness, light;
where there is sadness, joy;
for your mercy's and your truth's sake. Amen.

(Francis of Assisi)

Prayer help. The following are suggestions about how to be a healing presence:

For healing emotions or interpersonal relations. In your imagination see the scene or situation for which you want healing. Ask Jesus how he would handle the situation. Then ask him how he would want you to handle it. Let Jesus take your hand and lead you mentally into the situation and coach you in handling it properly. Take time, see the details. Be open to how you feel about Jesus' helping you. Repeat this mental imaging and meditating several times and for several days, until you think that you are ready to try it on your own in your life.

For healing a bodily disease. Relax by doing stretching exercises and deep breathing. In your mind, sense that the diseased organ is curing itself, or being cured. Sense how it would be and how it would feel when cured. Now, image and feel it happening. Imagine the white cells or healing forces rushing toward the area. As you breathe in, breathe in God's healing energy to the affected spot. And as you exhale, breathe out the poison that hinders healing. Do not order the healing to happen, but suggest expectantly that it is happening through Jesus' power. Do this for five minutes at a time, three times a day. It is also helpful to have others pray for you and with you.

For healing others. Some people have a healing voice, a gentle touch, or an affirming way of dealing with people in the frictions of life. Others can cultivate these qualities. To affirm others can also be very healing and can be cultivated. So can a certain interpersonal warmth and an interest and liking for others. People can often tell a lot from your tone of voice alone. Reflect on recent encounters with people. Were you a healing presence to them through your greeting? by the positive nature of your response to them? by your gestures and body language? through helpful action?

Reflection 7

Jesus, Prayerful

Presence. Try to relax, put aside the cares of the day, and abide in God's loving care. God is near.

Focus. How satisfied are you with your praying? How would you like it to be different?

Jesus, Prayerful

[Jesus] was praying in a certain place, and after he had finished, one of his disciples said to him, . . . "Teach us to pray." (Luke 11:1)

Comment

Like every devout Jew, Jesus undoubtedly said prescribed morning and evening prayers. But, different from common custom, he also prayed many other times informally: on the mountain, in a lonely spot, outside the town, at night.

Given the strains of his intense life, Jesus found retreat into prayer essential to keeping his balance and doing the main thing: God's will—the loving thing for the sake of the divine Reign. In prayer, Jesus could also savor his *Abba's* (Father's) presence and comfort, gather strength and joy, and keep his vision clear.

Openings for Prayer

In your imagination, go along with Jesus outside the town, to the mountain, or to some lonely spot. Try to picture the scene in great detail. Sit, stand, or kneel with him, and ask to pray with him. How did he pray? What do you think were his sentiments of mind and heart?

Talk about your own prayer life with Jesus, about what you desire it to be like.

Asking God for relief from pain or some evil is surely worthy prayer. What are some other ways of praying and some other subjects for Christian prayer?

Group Reflection and Sharing

What does the Scripture passage suggest about Jesus?

For people who like to pray, something makes it a joy. What do you think it is?

Doing some praying in set-aside time is advantageous, if not absolutely necessary, to living a focused spiritual life and nourishing a love for Jesus. Pool your experiences about finding set-aside times. When, where, and how do you find them? Be imaginative!

Ponder this question: Is Christ calling everyone to set aside time, sacred time, to converse with him on a regular basis?

What helps or hinders your efforts to pray?

"I'd like to pray more, but I am so busy!" Is this true of you? What can you do to make time for prayer?

Closing. Make or renew a commitment to a time and place for prayer during the next week.

Offer any intentions that come from your heart.

Prayer. Divine and hidden friend, I often feel that I fail at prayer, but I rejoice that your Spirit prays ceaselessly in my heart. Grant me the grace to sit still that I may hear the Spirit's song, ever flowing like a river deep within, singing my love for you.

Quiet my restless heart,
      calm my roving, runaway mind,
      as now, in communion with all the earth
      and her many-colored children,
      I enter into the song of love,
      the prayer of stillness.

                (Hays, *Prayers for a Planetary Pilgrim*, p. 97)

Prayer help. Everything in life is a gift from God. Gratitude and praise are the most natural responses to the giftedness of life. Praising God even in the bad times can plant the seeds of joy in our heart. The root of joy is gratefulness and praise.

This prayer from the Syrian Eucharistic Preface may be said, sung, or proclaimed in praise of God's goodness and glory. It is intended for the soul longing for the infinite and longing to shout or sing "Glory," "Praise," and "Honor." As you pray the "Eucharistia," mentally accompany it with full symphony, large choir, and a great organ!

Right indeed is it and just, that we should give thanks to [you],
Glorify [you] and praise [you], God, . . . of heaven and earth.
Together with [your] Incarnate Son and the Holy Spirit.
[yours], O God, are all creatures in heaven and earth
    and they incessantly glorify [you].
The sun heralds [you], the moon reveres [you]
    and all celestial bodies highly praise [you].
The seas extoll [you] and everything that is in them.
The earth, truly [your] footstool, worships [you].
She glorifies [your] Godhead in the Holy Church, who offers
    pure hymns through the mouth of [your] children:
Through the foretelling of prophets,
Through the hosts of apostles,
Through the death and stoning of martyrs,
Through the last breath of confessors,
Through the wisdom of doctors,
Through the glorious virtues of hermits,
Through the burden and toil of those who suffer poverty
    voluntarily,
Through the number of the just,
Through the joyous songs of virgins,
Through the sighs of those who suffer persecution,
Through the tears of penitents,
Further through every generation of the faithful.
The heavens also praise [you], arranged in three hierarchies;
There [you are] extolled, exalted, and praised:
Through psalms ever renewed,
Through pure and holy hymns,

Through the sweet sounds of the harp and delightful songs of
   praise,
Through triumphant and solemn chants, never silent and
   never ending,
Through the glowing flames of fiery voices,
Where thousand times thousand and myriad times myriad
   sing perpetual hymns of praise,
Not with human but with flaming tongues . . .
Through the sweetest melodies of angels,
Through the jubilant harmonies of archangels,
Through the sonorous voices of Principalities,
Through the splendour of Powers,
Through the awe-inspiring calls of Dominations,
Through the warriors of the heavenly Virtues,
Through the most elect canticles of the Thrones,
Through the fearful thunder of the Cherubim,
Through the burning wings of the six-winged Seraphim,
Who sing, cry, shout and speak forever with one and the same
   voice of Jubilation:
          Holy! Holy! Holy!
       (Shrady, ed., *Come, South Wind*, pp. 151–152)

Reflection 8

Jesus Sees Through the Darkness

Presence. God is near and all around us. Try to be more gladly aware of God's abiding presence.

Focus. What areas or circumstances in your life are most likely to generate stress or worry?

Jesus Sees Through the Darkness

"Do not worry about your life, what you will eat, or about your body, what you will wear. For life is more than food, and the body more than clothing. Consider the ravens: they neither sow nor reap, they have neither storehouse nor barn, and yet God feeds them. Of how much more value are you than the birds! . . . Consider the lilies, how they grow: they neither toil nor spin; yet I tell you, even Solomon in all his glory was not clothed like one of these. But if God so clothes the grass of the field, which is alive today and tomorrow is thrown into the oven, how much more will he clothe you—you of little faith! . . . Do not keep worrying. For it is the nations of the world that strive after all these things. . . . Instead, strive for [God's Reign], and these things will be given to you as well." (Luke 12:22–31)

Comment

As his journey led toward Jerusalem, Jesus experienced a most difficult call: the call to live in blind faith and trust. He had to walk holding onto God's hand, not knowing how it would all work out. If ever anyone had trust in God, complete trust right to the end, it was Jesus.

Openings for Prayer

Is there some problem—or maybe several—that you think Jesus would be happy to have you turn over to God, and then, relaxed, go ahead and plod on in faith—doing what you can and leaving the final results to God? God and you ride tandem on the journey of life. Is it time to let God sit up front and steer?

Would sharing your burden or anxiety with a friend help you carry your difficulties more easily?

If things do not work out, if a patient dies or poverty strikes, does this mean that trust in God was in vain? What advice would Jesus give you about this?

Group Reflection and Sharing

What thoughts or feelings does the passage suggest about Jesus?

In life's bleak periods, what pulls you through? Is God to be found in such darkness?

Are you experiencing any darkness that you would welcome talking about?

What does trust in God mean? What are we to make of trusting God when we ask over and over but seem to get no response?

What would happen if we decided to trust as Jesus did?

What might Jesus' words mean for poor people?

Closing. Does this meditation offer any helpful advice for your everyday life?

Offer any intentions that are close to your heart.

Prayer. God of fidelity and compassion, you have always been there for your people: for the Hebrews, for Jesus, and for us. May we seek and find your presence in dark times as well as in light times. Teach us that spirituality is not a do-it-yourself project. Teach us to trust your love and care in every circumstance, remembering your goodness from age to age and even until now. Amen.

Prayer help. When bringing problems to Jesus, be sure to use your own words for all the bitter or anxious feelings in your heart as well as the hopeful and positive ones. He will understand both. This is how one talks with a friend. And such openness better prepares you to receive God's peace, which, in the midst of anxiety and even tragedy, surpasses all understanding.

Reflection 9

Jesus, Compassionately Forgiving

Presence. Become physically relaxed and at ease. Then ask God to bless this period you want to spend together.

Focus. Who are the "tax collectors and sinners" of our time? When you encounter one of them, how do you feel?

Jesus, Compassionately Forgiving

All the tax collectors and sinners were coming near to listen to [Jesus]. And the Pharisees and the scribes were grumbling and saying, "This fellow welcomes sinners and eats with them."

So he told them this parable: "Which one of you, having a hundred sheep and losing one of them, does not leave the ninety-nine in the wilderness and go after the one that is lost until he finds it? When he has found it, he lays it on his shoulders and rejoices. And when he comes home, he calls together his friends and neighbors, saying to them, 'Rejoice with me, for I have found my sheep that was lost.' Just so, I tell you, there will be more joy in heaven over one sinner who repents than over ninety-nine righteous persons who need no repentance." (Luke 15:1–7)

Comment

It is good that God is compassionate because, when all is said and done, we strive for fine ideals and yet so frequently we do not reach them. Thankfully Jesus has decided to love us and to encourage us to keep trying anyway. Even though we rise and fall—we go up two steps but fall back one, and sometimes go up one but fall back two— Jesus keeps saying: "You can rely on my love and mercy. You will always have them. You cannot fail in life—if you just keep trying to live for me. So be not afraid."

Remember that forgiveness is in the intention and action, not necessarily in the feelings. When we intend to and try to act compassionately, our feelings may eventually and gradually come into harmony, too.

Opening for Prayer

Is forgiving certain people a problem for you? If so, carry these people to Jesus for a serious conversation.

Talk with Jesus about the matter on a larger scale. Does Jesus call the United States to forgive Japan for the bombing of Pearl Harbor and its aftermath? Is Japan supposed to forgive the United States for the bombing of Hiroshima? Are victims of the Holocaust supposed to forgive Hitler?

Group Reflection and Sharing

What does the Scripture passage suggest about Jesus?

What helps you act with compassion, or at least benevolence, toward people you may not like?

How do we learn compassion and forgiveness toward people of different races or socioeconomic classes?

Does forgiveness need limits? Consider what the Lord's Prayer allows.

Can you think of an example of how forgiveness can be marvelously helpful? Or another way of reflecting on this would be to ask, What happens to us when we refuse to forgive?

Christians are to struggle with social evils and human rights violations by enduring and forgiving as well as by direct action. How does one decide which approach is most appropriate? Select an example for discussion.

What can be done when it is extremely hard to forgive someone who has hurt you?

Does this meditation suggest to you any idea for action?

Closing. Recall an incident in which you felt slighted by someone. Hold that person's image before you as you pray.

Offer any intentions that come from your heart.

Prayer. Compassionate God, you never fail to love us where we are, to invite and welcome us into your presence. Teach us to be, as you are, a compassionate presence to all sinners in our world, including ourselves. In Jesus' name we pray. Amen.

Prayer help. Keep watching for things you admire in Jesus or things that draw you to love him. Tell him about these things. And once again, if it is hard to find time to pray, read early in the morning and mull things over during the day.

Reflection 10

Jesus, Zealous

Presence. Thank God for this chance to be in the presence of the Holy One. Try to grow calm and sense that God is near.

Focus. On this scale, where do you place yourself?
Workaholic . . . . . . Balanced . . . . . . Chronic couch potato

Jesus, Zealous

Jesus told his followers: "A prominent man took a trip to a distant land. Before he left, he distributed sums of money among ten of his servants, telling them to invest the money while he was gone.

When he returned home, he asked for an accounting. The first servant had doubled the amount he had been given. "Well done," the employer replied. "Since you did so well in such a minor matter, I put you in charge of ten villages."

The next servant had earned half-again what he had been given. "Fine," said the employer, "You get the management of five villages."

The third servant gave his report: "I hid your money because I was afraid of what you might do if I lost it. Here, Sir, is your money back just as you gave it to me." To him, the employer declared, "You incompetent! Why didn't you loan the money with interest or do something to multiply what I gave you?" (Adapted from Luke 19:11–27)

Comment

One way of stating the message of this passage is, "Use your time well." But what does that mean? Does every ordinary, playful, time-killing action have to be justified? Did not Jesus, and cannot we, "come away . . . and rest a while" (Mark 6:31)? On the other hand, anything can get out of balance, so how do we find the right balance between zeal and calm, work and recreation, and so on?

If recreation helps us pray, do our duties, love God and neighbor, or somehow fits us for the work of God's Reign, then it really is re-creating, a worthy endeavor. By the same token, if work loses its focus, becomes compulsive, and is damaging to people, then Jesus would not consider it to be Christian zeal. Maybe the key question is, Does whatever I am doing or not doing build God's Reign?

Openings for Prayer

This age-old question still retains its relevance: If you knew that you had just a week to live, how would you spend your time?

Saint John Berchmans, when asked what he would do if he were going to die in an hour, reportedly replied, "Just what I am doing." (He was playing billiards.) Your thoughts? How would you answer?

What benefit have you gained from the last ten reflections on the traits of Jesus? Have you come to know Jesus better? Perhaps you could review the meditations and talk with him about this.

Group Reflection and Sharing

What does the Scripture passage suggest about Jesus?

It is not always easy to keep up enthusiasm for using one's giftedness in everyday life. Becoming burned out and tired is all too easy! Are these conditions preventable or inevitable?

What do you think helped Jesus maintain his enthusiasm for God's work?

Consider how the following activities can and do fit in to making a world of love of God and neighbor: cooking, fine arts, sports, economics, office work, TV watching, sleeping, visiting, cutting the lawn.

Have you had experiences that you would care to share of success, failure, or burnout in trying to do some good?

Some people spend countless hours enthusiastically following professional sports, soap operas, or talk shows! And some young people do the same with video games. Comments?

Does this meditation suggest any idea for action?

Closing. Thérèse of Lisieux, Catherine McAuley, Dorothy Day, and Mother Teresa placed great stress on the "Little Way," or doing the ordinary extraordinarily well—with love. They all understood that even small acts, done lovingly, can be the secret to holiness. And when a person feels that everything she or he does is for Jesus or God, everything takes on a deeper meaning. Even the simplest tasks become sources of inner contentment. What do you think? Does this make sense in your experience?

Offer any intentions that come from your heart.

Prayer.

O eternal and compassionate God, in your wisdom you created humanity and told us to steward your creation. . . . Give us wisdom so that we may do what is just and good. Your divine wisdom knows all and comprehends everything. Wisdom will guide all our endeavors with moderation and enfold us in wisdom's protecting power. Amen. (Adapted from Wisdom 9:1–4,10–11)

Part 2:

Jesus and the Many Ways of Our Love

Introduction

Try not to leave the ten reflections in part 2 until you sense the several ways in which Jesus would like to relate to you. They will be unfolded gradually through texts from John. These reflections can help to deepen your love.

As preparation for the meditations, pause for a while to ask yourself: How do I relate to Jesus right now? Do I relate to Jesus as any of the following:

- the unsure person (*Jesus Christ Superstar*)
- the celebrating clown-figure (*Godspell*)
- the intense man whose time was too short for the urgent work that must be done (Passolini's *Gospel According to Matthew*)
- the suffering servant (Mark)
- the teacher and new Moses (Matthew)
- the friend to all: women, Gentiles, and especially outcasts (Luke)
- the person of prayer (Luke)
- the man whose last temptation was to withdraw from the struggle, marry Mary Magdalene, settle down, and watch the world from the comfort of his front porch (Kazantzakis)

- the resolute Jesus knowing only one thing: doing God's will regardless of cost (David Lean)
- he who challenges us to forgive, repent, celebrate, love, and trust (John Shea)
- the "Hound of Heaven" (Francis Thompson)
- the Way, the Truth, and the Life (John)
- the Good Shepherd, the Vine, the Son of God (John)
- the advocate and companion of the poor (Francis of Assisi)
- the man with a mission (Ignatius of Loyola)

Or do I relate to Jesus as one of the following:
- a stern Byzantine Christ
- a "fire and brimstone" Christ
- a saccharine-sweet, holy-picture Christ
- Christ, haloed, radiant, and gentle teacher
- Christ, long-faced with sorrow, crowned with thorns
- a haggard, disgruntled militant
- a teacher of love who becomes apocalyptic and fanatical
- one who gathers the lowly to start a marxist revolution
- a Jonathan Livingston Seagull Christ—you can become more and better than you are
- your brother and friend

What is your dominant image of Jesus? What attracts and stirs your love? Or is it none of the above, but a personal composite, perhaps intuitively formed after considering Jesus' qualities, as was done in part 1.

Reminders

For short periods of prayer, one possibility is to read, run, and mull. Read early in the morning, then reflect on the reading on your way to work and during the day.

For longer prayer periods, read the meditation through. Then let the Spirit take over. Pray over whatever thoughts or feelings come to mind. Especially let yourself be drawn into affective prayer: "Falling in love" is not too strong a phrase.

Most important, let yourself be drawn to Jesus with whatever your heart feels: with prayer of deep desire to know and be close to him, deep desire to live for and follow him, deep desire to be available and open to him. Talk as with an intimate friend. Talk very simply, perhaps with words of wonder and awe, thanks and praise, or sorrow and longing such as only love knows. Or talk with words of celebration; or petition; or grief that he is so little loved; or joy at Jesus' work, desire for intimacy, and desire for healing of personal hurts; or for the spread of God's Reign.

Feel free to voice your feelings about how the Scriptures apply to the world and people everywhere; and also to express negative feelings, frustration, impatience, anger, anxiety—all are appropriate material for prayer. For positive emotions it is helpful to repeat lovingly, several times, sentiments you enjoy. Tevye, the Jewish father in *Fiddler on the Roof*, might serve as a model of personal freedom in addressing God.

You could then begin to read the Scriptures or the whole meditation a second time—again slowly—and again pausing where you feel touched or moved.

After the reflection, notice how it has affected the way you feel and think about your relationship with Jesus. You could also notice whether it has changed the way you feel and think about your relationship with God the Creator or the Holy Spirit.

In part 2 each meditation is like going to prayer or discussion after having a visit with John the Evangelist, who has related some significant event in Jesus' life.

Reflection 11

Who Do You Say That Jesus Is?

Presence. O God, you are always close to us. May we always realize this.

Focus. Bring to mind and into focus your present, dominant image of Jesus. How do you know whether this image corresponds to Jesus as he really is?

Who Do You Say That Jesus Is?

In the beginning was the Word, and the Word was with God, and the Word was God. He was in the beginning with God. All things came into being through him, and without him not one thing came into being. What has come into being in him was life, and the life was the light of all people. The light shines in the darkness, and the darkness did not overcome it. . . .

He was in the world, and the world came into being through him; yet the world did not know him. He came to what was his own, and his own people did not accept him. But to all who received him, who believed in his name, he gave power to become children of God. . . .

And the Word became flesh and lived among us, and we have seen his glory, . . . full of grace and truth. (John 1:1–14)

Comment

Before we reflect on Jesus' ideas about our mutual relationship, we need to ask: Who is this person to whom I am relating? If Jesus has asked to be the most important person in my life, and if I am considering giving my consent, I would like to know who Jesus is.

Openings for Prayer

Reread the introduction to part 2 and consider the question: Who is he for me?

Pray in any way you can that you will grow in your love for Jesus Christ!

Linger affectionately over phrases of the Scripture passage from John 1:1–14. Hold passages in your heart and mind and taste them as you would if you were slowly savoring a tasty grape or orange.

Group Reflection and Sharing

What is the Scripture passage saying to you? What does it suggest about relating to Jesus?

Imagine: You are the fifth Evangelist, and you feel called by the Spirit to write a Gospel. Given your experience with Jesus, how would you begin your Gospel? What point of view about Jesus would you stress in writing for contemporary people? Remember that each of the four Gospel writers did take a particular point of view. For example, Matthew, writing for the Jews, presents Jesus as the new Moses and teacher of Israel. John, writing primarily for new Christians, presents Jesus as the divine Son of God.

If Jesus had not been divine but was otherwise exactly as we find him in the Scriptures, would it make any difference?

During certain parts of Christian history, Christ's divinity has been stressed; at other times, such as today, his humanity is stressed. Do we have the right balance?

How have your images of Jesus changed over the past ten years? What factors may have influenced any shifts?

Has this meditation invited any change in your view of Jesus?

Closing. Take a minute to refocus your image of Jesus in light of this meditation.

Offer any intentions that come from your heart.

Prayer. Jesus, you came from God to walk among us and to draw us to you. Show us your face that we may know you in truth and in love, as you are and as who you desire to be for us. Continue to make your presence known, now and always. Amen.

Prayer help. From this point on, you may want to conclude the reflections with heart-to-heart words with God the Creator as well as with Jesus.

Reflection 12

Jesus, Inviting

Presence. Stretch or breathe deeply to calm yourself. Recall God's support and nearness. Ask that your prayer be to God's honor and glory.

Focus. How would Jesus like to relate to us? What are the roles he sees us playing, one to the other?

Jesus, Inviting

The next day John again was standing with two of his disciples, and as he watched Jesus walk by, he exclaimed, "Look, here is the Lamb of God!" The two disciples heard him say this, and they followed Jesus. When Jesus turned and saw them following, he said to them, "What are you looking for?" They said to him, "Rabbi" (which translated means Teacher), "where are you staying?" He said to them, "Come and see." They came and saw where he was staying, and they remained with him that day. It was about four o'clock in the afternoon. (John 1:35–39)

Comment

How would Jesus like to relate to you? What are the roles he sees us playing, one to the other? Jesus gives us some answers to these questions in the next eight reflections. First, the Teacher invites us to "Come and see!" Like most relationships, this one begins with an invitation.

Openings for Prayer

In your mind's eye, go back to Palestine and walk along with James and John as companions over the dusty clay roads. With all the power of your imagination, see Jesus being pointed out to you by an itinerant preacher, John the Baptist, who says, "Look, there is the Lamb of God!" Along with the two curious disciples, you begin to follow Jesus. He unexpectedly turns and says, "What are you looking for?" Caught by surprise, you stumble out with, "Where do you live?" "Come and see," he replies, looking straight at you. What thoughts and feelings are you having?

Ponder this: Yours are the only hands, heart, head, and voice that Jesus has today! You are invited to work, suffer, love, and pray in his stead. How do you feel about this? What challenges and opportunities do you have?

Group Reflection and Sharing

What does the Scripture passage suggest about relating to Jesus?

When we recognize that Jesus is asking us to "come and see," how might this affect us?

Does sensing one's dignity in being invited by Jesus bring personal advantages? Or, in all honesty, does it feel like a burden?

Of course the disciples were ultimately being invited to work with Jesus, to join his ministry. What is your experience of working at jobs or projects with others? How would it be like and unlike working with Jesus?

Knowing what you do about Jesus, draw up a list of ten guiding principles for Christian work. Try to attach each principle to a parable by, a saying from, or a story about Jesus.

As coworkers with Jesus, most of us have decided limitations—to put it mildly. In choosing the likes of us to "come and see" and to be coworkers, what do you think God had in mind?

Does this meditation suggest any ideas for working with Jesus in your job, your community, or your role in life?

Closing. Picture again Jesus' loving look as he invites you to "come and see."

Offer any intentions that come from your heart.

Prayer. Jesus, from the beginning of your ministry you invited others to share your life and your work. Help us to be attentive to your call. Shape us, mold us, and put us to work in your vineyards. Amen.

Prayer help. Why not talk with Jesus your Coworker or with God the Creator during the day as well as at prayer?

Reflection 13

Jesus, A Celebrating Friend

Presence. Grow quiet inwardly and become receptive to the Spirit's inspirations.

Focus. Have your ever thought of Jesus as a friend who is enjoying play and recreation along with you? How does it feel to consider that possibility?

Jesus, A Celebrating Friend

There was a wedding in Cana of Galilee, and the mother of Jesus was there. Jesus and his disciples had also been invited to the wedding. When the wine gave out, the mother of Jesus said to him, "They have no wine." . . . His mother said to the servants, "Do whatever he tells you." Now standing there were six stone water jars for the Jewish rites of purification, each holding twenty or thirty gallons. Jesus said to them, "Fill the jars with water." And they filled them up to the brim. He said to them, "Now draw some out, and take it to the chief steward." . . . When the steward tasted the water that had become wine, . . . the steward called the bridegroom and said to him, "Everyone serves the good wine first, and then the inferior wine after the guests have become drunk. But you have kept the good wine until now." (John 2:1–10)

Comment

The story ends by saying, "this, the first of his signs, . . . revealed his glory" (John 2:11). Jesus certainly showed his power for good, but the passage also suggests a sense of humor. Imagine how nonplussed people were, at least those sober enough, when they drank fine wine far into the celebration. Indeed, many stories in the Gospels show Jesus eating and drinking with all sorts of people. He also chose a banquet, the Last Supper, for one of the key revelations dur

ing his earthly life. Jesus, human and divine, knew how important celebrations are to living fully.

Openings for Prayer

Sometimes people misread the Scriptures and look at God as oppressive or anti-joy. From the story of the wedding feast at Cana, we see Jesus fostering human happiness. For Christians it is okay to be happy, to celebrate, to revel in natural goodness! Do you find such a Jesus a challenge or a consolation?

> If I had my life to live over, I'd like to make more mistakes next time. I'd relax. I would be sillier. . . . I would take fewer things seriously. I would take more chances. I would climb more mountains and swim more rivers. I would eat more ice cream and less beans. I would start barefoot earlier in the Spring and stay that way later in the Fall. I would go to more dances. I would ride more merry-go-rounds. I would pick more daisies than on this trip. (Nadine Stair, Louisville, Kentucky, 85 years old)

What do you want to start doing, so that at eighty-five years of age you will have few regrets?

Group Reflection and Sharing

What does the Scripture passage suggest about relating to Jesus?

Can a typical Saturday night party be a religious experience? How about national celebrations? For example, what thoughts and feelings might course through your mind and heart if you are part of the Times Square pandemonium on New Year's Eve? Can you think of Jesus as being there and enjoying it? What might he be thinking or feeling?

We "celebrate" sacraments. What does this mean?

How can we grow to sense that Jesus is near us in our good times?

Deep in human nature lies an instinct to celebrate even when things are at their worst. What are we to make of this joyous instinct?

Should all of us celebrate more?

Does this meditation suggest any idea for action?

Closing. What is there about your experience as a Christian that gives you reason to celebrate with Jesus?

Offer any intentions that are in your heart.

Prayer

Sing out your joy to the Creator, good people;
for praise is fitting for loyal hearts.
Give thanks to the Creator upon the harp,
with a ten-stringed lute sing songs.
O sing a new song;
play skillfully and loudly so all may hear.
For the word of the Creator is faithful,
and all God's works are to be trusted.
The Creator loves justice and right
and fills the earth with faithful love.

(Psalm 33:1–5)

Prayer help. Some ideas for celebrating with Jesus—some ideas follow:

In daily life. Ask yourself: How shall I find you, Jesus, in the "party" of everyday life, in the things I like to do, and in the people I like to be with? Attend to them; listen with the heart. For prayer, revel in the gift of existence, in the gift of each of your senses in turn. Then do the same for your mind and its special abilities, and for your heart, for its abilities. For celebratory passages from the Scriptures, see Philippians 4:4, Psalms 32, 84, 87, and 119. Better yet, get into the regular practice of composing your own hymns of thanks, praise, and celebration.

While working.
- Talk with Jesus as you work.
- Sing hymns or let them float in your mind.
- Say the Jesus Prayer ("Jesus Christ, Son of God, have mercy on me, a sinner").
- Reverently repeat the name of Jesus.
- Say a morning offering when you leave the house or enter the workplace.
- Offer new tasks to God.
- Thank God for little things and little ones.
- Rejoice in being a parent, a spouse, a member of your family, a worker.
- Praise God for blessings; yes, and for crosses too!
- Keep an end-of-the-day list for the little gifts that come your way each day, and pray the list to God each evening.

In marriage. Is this a day to emphasize more the beauty, delicacy, and mystery of sexual and marital joy? Sexual joy is a foretaste of companionship and ecstatic union with God. And remember: Nothing brings joy to marriage like little acts of thoughtfulness, little generosities, little signs of affection. How often do you say "thank-you" to the one you love?

Reflection 14

Jesus, Allowing Love to Grow Slowly

Presence. Do what you are doing. Prepare to enter into prayer with that spirit.

Focus. When did you first meet Jesus? How has your relationship developed?

Jesus, Allowing Love to Grow Slowly

A Samaritan woman came to draw water, and Jesus said to her, "Give me a drink." . . . The Samaritan woman said to him, "How is it that you, a Jew, ask a drink of me, a woman of Samaria?" . . . Jesus answered her, "If you knew the gift of God, and who it is that is saying to you, 'Give me a drink,' you would have asked him, and he would have given you living water." The woman said to him, "Sir, you have no bucket and the well is deep. Where do you get that living water?" . . . Jesus said to her, "Everyone who drinks of this water will be thirsty again, but those who drink of the water that I will give them will never be thirsty. The water that I will give will become in them a spring of water gushing up to eternal life." The woman said to him, "Sir, give me this water, so that I may never be thirsty or have to keep coming here to draw water."

Jesus said to her, "Go, call your husband, and come back." The woman answered him, "I have no husband." Jesus said to her, "You are right in saying, 'I have no husband'; for you have had five husbands, and the one you have now is not your husband. What you have said is true!" The woman said to him, "Sir, I see that you are a prophet. Our ancestors worshiped on this mountain, but you say that the place where people must worship is in Jerusalem." Jesus said to her, "Woman, believe me, the hour is coming when you will worship . . . neither on this mountain nor in Jerusalem." (John 4:7–21)

Comment

Jesus sits down with this outcast woman and does not badger or press her. He accepts her where she is. He simply invites her to look deeper into life's meaning. This is a great service that we can do for one another. We can invite one another to share our stories. In the telling come new insights and, hopefully, a bonding in friendship. Even when the woman changes the subject of the conversation, Jesus stays with her, accepting her as she is. Jesus does the same for us. He does not insist on instant conversion, but goes along as far as he can with us at the moment.

Openings for Prayer

Is your relationship with Jesus progressing as you would like? What can you do that might give it more of a chance?

If, like the woman, you were to have a five-minute conversation with Jesus right now, how do you think the conversation might flow? Try carrying on this conversation in your imagination or by writing the dialog.

Imagine living an ordinary day with deeper than ordinary love in your heart. What might it be like and feel like doing one of your usual activities with more love?

Group Reflection and Sharing

What does the Scripture passage suggest about relating to Jesus?

What is your experience of how relationships develop? Could you see a relationship with God or Jesus passing through similar stages?

Do you ever feel that you are not growing fast enough spiritually? The important question is, How can you do so? Any suggestions?

Do you think love of God can deepen without one's noticing it? Theologian Karl Rahner would say that enduring and persistent faithfulness to daily duties would be a sure sign of such growth. Is this observation of some comfort?

When it seems that God is distant, the conventional wisdom of the saints is to continue to pray anyway. If your spiritual life seems stagnant for some time, talk with someone learned in the spiritual life. What other sources of spiritual growth can you tap?

Does your reflection suggest an idea for action?

Closing. Become aware that Jesus desires a relationship with you—as he did with the Samaritan woman.

Offer any intentions that are in your heart.

Prayer. I want to talk to you, Jesus, just as if you are standing beside me. I want to tell you face-to-face how much I love you. Give me courage to accept your acceptance of me. Give me patience to persevere in wanting you. May I hear your voice when you say,

"Arise, my love . . .
and come away;
for now the winter is past,
the rain is over and gone."

(Song of Solomon 2:10)

Reflection 15

Jesus, Guiding Light

Presence. God is near, so we can relax in holy love and divine presence.

Focus. Clarity about how to live our life does not usually come instantly or easily. Recall some persons, events, or circumstances that have contributed to your growth in insight and understanding about your own life.

Jesus, Guiding Light

[Jesus] saw a man blind from birth. His disciples asked him, "Rabbi, who sinned, this man or his parents, that he was born blind?" Jesus answered, "Neither this man nor his parents sinned; he was born blind so that God's works might be revealed in him. We must work the works of him who sent me while it is day; night is coming when no one can work. As long as I am in the world, I am the light of the world." When he had said this, he spat on the ground and made mud with the saliva and spread the mud on the man's eyes, saying to him, "Go, wash in the pool of Siloam." Then he went and washed and came back able to see. (John 9:1–7)

Comment

Jesus made it clear that blindness, illness, and incapacities are not punishment for sin (a lesson many of us still need to learn from him). God's glory can be shown in all people if we but see the light of Christ in them. God's glory shines in us if we will open up the light of Christ in our own soul. Seeing the Christ-light and letting it guide us is a miracle of grace performed now as it has been for two thousand years.

Openings for Prayer

If you want more light on something—on who you are, why you are not getting the right reactions from people, why you are missing out on peace of mind or success, or why you are having problems—take these matters to Jesus. He will shed light on them.

Are you coming to love more intensely Jesus the Christ and his message of light about how to live? If so, how so? If not, why not?

So far in your meditations, what seems to be attracting you to Jesus in new ways?

Group Reflection and Sharing

What does this Scripture passage suggest about relating to Jesus?

Christ's light guides and strengthens us to cocreate God's Reign; we embrace what helps us do that, and we let go of what does not. How do you seek this light and comprehend it?

If you live in Christ's light and make cocreating God's Reign central to your life, how will that influence the way you vote? the way you treat children? the way you shop? work? endure suffering? watch the evening news?

If you live by Christ's light, will you feel more burdened or more free?

When struggling with a problem, reading the Scriptures and watching for any passage that might seem relevant can be a source of light. Favorite Scripture or literature passages offer light or support in difficult situations. Some people like to commit favorite passages to memory or to make personal collections of them. What are some issues about which these scriptural approaches might help you find Christ's light?

Closing. Reflect on these questions: In what area of my life do I need greater clarity about how to live right now? Does this need suggest any ideas for action?

Offer any intentions that come from your heart.

Prayer. Divine Light, I need all the light I can get. Thank you for sending Jesus as guide and counselor, lest I walk in darkness, feeling empty and without goals. Help me to be attentive, to listen with both mind and heart to your Son, the light of the world, who is in the world. Amen.

Prayer help. The Good News is that everything that we see in Christ, we find in God. We may approach God with simplicity like a child who cries "Daddy" or "Mommy" as he or she runs to meet a parent who returns from an absence. Many people today need to hear this news about God over and over.

Sometimes people are afraid of God. They think God is always peering around corners, taking notes, waiting for an opportunity to zap them. But we are God's children. And in the Scriptures, God's love is imaged as being stronger than even a mother's love. Like a loving parent, God gives light to show the way. In seeking Christ's light, keep the following points in mind:

Pray. Try to be open to God when you pray. Try to seek what God wants, and pray that God may help you to know it. Saints call this disposition indifference, or detachment, or complete openness to God, or spiritual freedom. Pray for light repeatedly and expectantly for some weeks. God is interested!

Write out the reasons for a certain choice in one column on a sheet of paper and the reasons against it in another. Do the same for the second possible choice and the third. Mull over the possible consequences each choice might have for you, for your loved ones, for the world, and for God's work. Add or subtract reasons when you get an insight. Read the list over occasionally, noting the relative importance or unimportance of each reason. One highly significant reason might outweigh the others.

Discern at the gut level. Hold the choices up before God in order: the first, the second, the third. As you do, notice whether deep in your soul you feel yourself moved: "This seems to be the one. This is true to the real me. This is the one that really ought to be. This is the one with which I'd like to walk with Jesus. This is the one that seems to bring peace." Then hold them up before God the Creator, then before the Spirit. How does it feel? The deep-down gut feeling, especially the feeling of peace in a choice, helps us to make tough decisions.

Study. Learn more about the matter. Get the facts. If necessary, consult widely. Tap the common sense of good people. Then try praying, writing out reasons (as before), and discerning again.

A note for a perplexed conscience. What if you have to make a choice when the evidence seems 51 percent pro and 49 percent con? The 51 percent choice is likely the better, but stay open to new data. And do not feel overly guilty if one decision is basically good, but you do not have quite the strength needed to reach for one that is even better. Just be honest with yourself and with Jesus, and maybe in due time the strength will come.

Reflection 16

Jesus, Savior and Blessed Assurance

Presence. God has loving concern for everyone. Sink into this loving care, and relax as you prepare for prayer.

Focus. In this life, as we know, there are parties and then there are parties. Imagine none other than God throwing the one and eternal party. Let your imagination run!

Jesus, Savior and Blessed Assurance

When Martha heard that Jesus was coming, she went and met him, while Mary stayed at home. Martha said to Jesus, "Lord, if you had been here, my brother would not have died. But even now I know that God will give you whatever you ask. . . . Jesus said to her, "Your brother will rise again." Martha said to him, "I know that he will rise again in the resurrection on the last day." Jesus said to her, "I am the resurrection and the life. Those who believe in me, even though they die, will live, and everyone who lives and believes in me will never die. Do you believe this?" She said to him, "Yes, Lord, I believe that you are the Messiah, the Son of God, the one coming into the world." (John 11:20–27)

Comment

Paul declared that eyes have never seen and ears have never heard the glory of eternal life with Christ. Of course it is impossible to sketch accurately the joys of eternal life. We can only imagine them. Age after age, belief in the Resurrection has sustained people, given them hope in desperate times. Indeed, unless Jesus had risen, he would be just one more forgotten crucified criminal. His Resurrection is the central event in the Christian story. He is the resurrection that is promised to us.

Openings for Prayer

Why not let your heart fill with thoughts and feelings about your resurrection? Speak with the Risen Christ as you are moved to do so.

"Then I saw a new heaven and a new earth; for the first heaven and the first earth had passed away, and the sea was no more. And I saw the holy city, the new Jerusalem . . . prepared as a bride adorned for her husband" (Revelation 21:1–2). What images, feelings, and beliefs do you have about this new heaven and new earth?

Group Reflection and Sharing

What comes to mind as you read the Scripture passage about relating to the Risen Christ?

Professing "Jesus Christ as my personal Lord and Savior" has become a formula for those who believe that they have been "born again" in Christ. What feelings and thoughts does this formula evoke in you? Is professing this belief enough?

To feel the impact of Jesus as savior, try to imagine living in Jesus' time when people had no assurance of life after death. Now leap ahead to our time. What would life be like if we too thought that death really was the end of existence?

The thought of eternal life very much comforts and supports people, especially poor and oppressed people. Many of the spirituals sung by slaves testify to this. But does this blessed assurance of the resurrection mean that Christians need not work for social justice?

How much do thoughts of death or heaven motivate Christians today?

Should the idea of merit be stressed more today in preaching and spiritual writing? Merit suggests that the more we love and serve God here, the more we will participate in his divine life forever.

Does this meditation offer any ideas for use in everyday life?

Closing. Reflect: You are invited to the greatest celebration! Let your heart respond.

Offer any intentions that come from your heart.

Prayer

Sing a new song to Yahweh,
who has done wonderful deeds,
whose right hand and whose holy arm
have brought salvation.
. . . .
Sing praise to Yahweh all the earth;
ring out your joy.

(Psalm 98:1–4)

Prayer help. Occasionally crystallize the main insight of a meditation into a very short sentence for repeating during the day.

Reflection 17

Jesus, My Servant!

Presence. How blessed and fortunate we are, for God is near. Be aware, attend to the holy presence of God.

Focus. Answer the following multiple-choice questions:

- When someone does me an unexpected act of service, I feel (choose those that apply) (*a*) delighted, (*b*) embarrassed, (*c*) important, (*d*) resistant, (*e*) connected, (*f*) confused.
- When I am asked to do an act of service for someone else, I feel (same choices) . . .

Jesus, My Servant!

Jesus, knowing that . . . he had come from God and was going to God, got up from the table, took off his outer robe, and tied a towel around himself. Then he poured water into a basin and began to wash the disciples' feet and to wipe them. . . .

After he had washed their feet, had put on his robe, and had returned to the table, he said to them, "Do you know what I have done to you? You call me Teacher and Lord—and you are right, for that is what I am. So if I, your Lord and Teacher, have washed your feet, you also ought to wash one another's feet. For I have set you an example. (John 13:3–15)

Comment

Had a god ever before washed an earthling's feet? What shall we say when we reflect that *our* God is infinite, all-powerful, all-knowing, and omnipresent? Here Jesus takes the role of a slave in the culture of his time who, with no expectation of thanks, washed the guests' feet.

Openings for Prayer

The Creator, Savior, and Sustainer serves us all in each moment of existence. Respond with silence, a song, a dance, a play—whatever your heart urges you to do.

Talk with Christ about whose feet you should wash today, and about how to do so as graciously as he did.

For a reverent repetition of the meditation, in your imagination be part of the scene in John 13:1–17, and let Jesus wash your feet also.

Ponder this timeless teaching of Christ: Power and wealth are God-given endowments intended for serving our sisters and brothers. We are only stewards.

Group Reflection and Sharing

What does the Scripture passage suggest about relating to Jesus?

Any person can enrich his or her spiritual life by following Jesus as servant. Can you see why?

Recent theology describes one of the church's roles as that of servant-church. What are your thoughts about this? Do you think people see their parishes as communities of service?

What is your experience of being a servant?

People in service roles, such as maintenance people, waitresses, clerks, or auto mechanics, are often growled at by the public or spoken to sharply. Do you have comments on this?

How can Hollywood producers and stars and the rest of the "rich and famous" follow Jesus in his servant role?

Are parents to think of themselves as servants? Are children?

If business's primary aim really was service, what would happen?

What is being a servant supposed to mean for the ordinary person?

Closing. Reflect: Decide on one act of service you will do this week.

Offer any intentions that come from your heart.

Prayer. In our family and friends, in the poor and the lonely, in those scorned by our world, through the work that we do, through the commitments we keep, through our play and our joy, may our servant-lives witness to all you have done for us. Amen.

Reflection 18

Jesus, Merciful

Presence. Ask God's help to grow calm and to make this period fruitful.

Focus. The journey to deepened friendship with God has its ups and downs. In the silence of your heart, claim those times on your journey when you have wandered, stumbled, or become enamored of this or that and, for a time, forgotten about traveling.

Jesus, Merciful

The scribes and the Pharisees brought a woman who had been caught in adultery; and making her stand before all of them, they said to [Jesus], "Teacher, this woman was caught in the very act of committing adultery. Now in the law Moses commanded us to stone such women. Now what do you say?" . . . Jesus bent down and wrote with his finger on the ground. When they kept on questioning him, he straightened up and said to them, "Let anyone among you who is without sin be the first to throw a stone at her." . . . When they heard it, they went away, one by one, beginning with the elders; and Jesus was left alone with the woman standing before him. Jesus straightened up and said to her, "Woman, where are they? Has no one condemned you?" She said, "No one, sir." And Jesus said, "Neither do I condemn you. Go your way, and from now on do not sin again." (John 8:3–11)

Comment

When we have failed God or been listless or ignored God for a while, Jesus reveals the God of healing and tender mercy. Always. No matter how often! We can drop our guilt and be free to deal with our sins by starting over any number of times, seventy times seven if need be.

Openings for Prayer

Any reflections on Jesus always seem to come back to his mercy. Since it is a constant theme in the Jesus story, why should we not celebrate it again and again and again? How do you celebrate it?

What is the struggle or fault or reluctance about which you are most happy to enjoy God's mercy? Do you enjoy it?

The psalmists and the saints sing of God's enduring mercy. For your prayer, why not sing of God's mercies even now? God will forgive our off-key warbling, so cut loose!

Have you noticed how the number of good things about loving and following Jesus keeps growing?

Group Reflection and Sharing

What does the Scripture passage suggest about relating to Jesus?

Do you ever wonder whether the best way, if not the only way, for all of us to survive in an often cruel and unjust world is to try to be good and decent persons ourselves, and then to be everlastingly forgiving to those who are not? Or will the world then only get worse because everyone will take advantage? Isn't that our fear? But what do you think Jesus would want?

How can we best handle those mean feelings that make forgiving so hard?

"Forgive us as we forgive others." What could that mean for some local or personal problem?

When you think of forgiving yourself, what comes to mind? We usually think of forgiving others, but have we been missing something?

All over the world people seek freedom from oppression. Ideally, what attitudes will they try to take to their oppressors or former oppressors if following Jesus is a high priority? No one ever said Christianity was easy!

A deep and secret satisfaction comes from forgiving enemies. Have you ever had this joy? Recall the story of what happened.

Does this meditation suggest some resolution or practice?

Closing. Reflect on the last few lines of the Gospel passage. How might the woman have felt after she left Jesus? Try to identify with her feelings.

Offer any intentions that are in your heart.

Prayer. I thank you for accepting me where I am, merciful God, and for your constant forgiveness. I thank you for the transgressions of others that I may have the opportunity to forgive them as you have forgiven me. Make me aware of when I need to ask forgiveness from others. I pray this through your Son, Jesus. Amen.

Prayer help. Sin is a blight committed by individuals and by groups. Our individual sins make us less human, whether they are from uncharitable thinking, preoccupation with erotica, committing violence in the streets, intemperance in eating and drinking, stealing, or talking about people deprecatingly. Sin weakens our loving relationships. It wastes time and could shorten a lifespan and so cut short the work we could do for a friend. The cost of discipleship is the cost of following Jesus while in the throes of struggling against such sin. We fail often, yet we take literally Jesus' promise of everlasting forgiveness, then summon the courage to continue the struggle right in the midst of the grief that sin has unleashed in the world—just as Jesus did.

Communal sin is as old as humankind. It happens whenever one group oppresses or enslaves another. It also exists when one group has more than enough food and material goods, but another lacks necessaries for staying alive. Sin is not in the fact that one group has more than the other; the crucial factor is that one group has so much more than it needs while the other has not enough to live.

The difficult questions we agonize over and struggle with are these: What about people who know about such social evils and human rights violations, yet do not denounce them? Is that a sin of omission? What of those who participate in evils, such as investing in companies with unjust, unsafe labor practices? What of those who build up huge surpluses while so many others live in misery? What does Jesus think our responsibilities are to brothers and sisters who subsist on garbage, cannot find work, or are too sick to work?

These are probably the most difficult, agonizing, painful, and confronting questions the Gospels ask. And understandably so.

Jesus does tell the woman not to sin anymore. He tells us that, too. Blessedly, Jesus also forgives those who seek forgiveness and a change of heart.

Reflection 19

Jesus' Desire for Intimacy

Presence. Pause to grow calm and quiet. Decide to leave aside other concerns and enter with a glad spirit into this period.

Focus. What are some of the delights of intimacy as I have experienced them? What are some of intimacy's demands?

Jesus' Desire for Intimacy

I will not leave you orphaned; I am coming to you. . . .
     You are my friends. . . . I do not call you servants . . . but I have called you friends, because I have made known to you everything that I have heard. . . . You did not choose me but I chose you. (John 14:18; 15:14–16)

Comment

Intimacy means that in a relationship we leave ourselves open to being changed by the relationship. Jesus seeks such intimacy with us. Jesus has decided to be physically, attentively present to each person who would like his undivided attention. Jesus has not left us orphaned. We are his friends. When we gather at worship and share the Eucharist, when we love one another in small acts of kindness, when we read the word of God, we celebrate this intimacy.

Openings for Prayer

Draw the top of your dining room table. Draw a plate at each place at the table. Imagine that you have invited your six or eight most intimate family members and friends to dinner. Write their names on the plates. Then ponder this question: How intimate do you get with these people?

How intimate are you with Jesus?

Do worship and the Eucharist enhance your intimacy with Jesus?

To what kind of closeness do you think Jesus is calling you? Do you feel free to ask him that question?

Group Reflection and Sharing

What does the Scripture passage suggest about relating to Jesus?

Can something help to highlight our sense of intimacy with Jesus at the weekly worship in our church?

The following is a traditional, formal thanksgiving prayer:

> Heart of Jesus, think on me; Eyes of Jesus, look on me;
> Face of Jesus, shine on me; Hands of Jesus, bless me;
> Feet of Jesus, guide me; Arms of Jesus, hold me;
> Body of Jesus, feed me; Blood of Jesus, cleanse me;
> Make me, Jesus, your own, here; and in the world to come.

Does this prayer express your desire for intimacy? What elements of a prayer would speak to your desire for intimacy?

Do you have some favorite informal ways that help you find a sense of closeness to Christ?

Are some people secretly desirous of intimacy with Jesus, but also a little afraid? Where do fears of such intimacy come from?

If we are not intimate with other people, does this affect our intimacy with Jesus? Are there parallels between human intimacy and intimacy with Jesus?

Closing. Reflect: What are some of the delights and demands of intimacy with Jesus?

Offer any intentions that come from your heart.

Prayer. Thank you for calling me to you, Jesus. I want to be your intimate friend. Use me as an example of your love. Thank you, Jesus.

Prayer help. Concluding your prayer periods and receptions of the Eucharist with short, heart-to-heart conversations with Jesus will breed closeness. So will freely expressing feelings, both positive and negative. Meditating on the Gospels is a way of listening over and over again to your divine friend's story.

Reflection 20

Jesus' Further Desire

Presence. Quiet yourself in the calm of God's presence.

Focus. How do you feel when you know yourself to be truly accepted and loved? What difference do acceptance and love make in your life?

Jesus' Further Desire

"Those who love me will be loved by my Father, and I will love them and reveal myself to them. . . . We will come to them and make our home with them." (John 14:21–23)

"Pray then in this way: Our Father . . . " (Matthew 6:9)

Comment

Hear God saying: "Remember who you are: you are my child, that is who you are, no matter what, no matter what you have done, no matter what problem you have, no matter what sins you may have committed. You are my daughter. You are my son. Alleluia. Alleluia."

If we remember and accept this fact, we will realize that we are everyone's equal. We are a royal family who need envy no one.

Openings for Prayer

What thought could be happier than that God—our father, mother, lover, and so much more—really cares about each of us? Pray and talk with Christ about this as you feel inclined.

What have you found to be beneficial in the ten reflections of part 2? Have they enhanced your love for Jesus? If you wish, review the meditations to refresh your heart and mind about what you found most helpful.

Group Reflection and Sharing

What does the Scripture passage suggest about relating to Jesus?

Intimacy with God—what does this mean?

What has been your notion of God at different periods in your life? your notion of intimacy with God?

Believing that God, the father-mother of us all, invites each person into intimacy is difficult. Ancient gods were supposed to be indifferent to humans, and certainly not intimate. Yet this invitation comes from our Creator, the infinite one! What do you think God has in mind?

The Scriptures speak of God as both mother and father. Have you gotten accustomed to this enlarged idea of God's richness? It has many advantages—personal and social. What are some that come to mind?

The name that Jesus used for "Father" was actually *Abba*, meaning "Daddy" or "Pop"—clearly an affectionate, intimate name. Try praying the Lord's Prayer, starting with "Our Daddy" or "Our Pop." See how that feels. Then try "Our Mommy" or "Our Mom." What sort of intimacy does this give the prayer?

Do you think God's awesome omnipotence stands in the way of intimacy?

How might you cultivate intimacy with God in some practical way?

Closing. Spend a minute or so desiring God, or at least asking for that desire.

Offer any intentions that are in your heart.

Prayer

O God, you are my God whom I eagerly seek;
for you my flesh longs and my soul thirsts
like the earth, parched, lifeless, and without water.
I have gazed toward you in the sanctuary
to see your power and your glory.
For your love is better than life;
my lips shall glorify you.
Thus will I praise you while I live;

lifting up my hands, I will call upon your name.
My soul clings to you;
your right hand upholds me.

(Psalm 63:1–8)

Part 3:
Following Jesus by a Christian Life

Introduction

In view of all that Jesus has done for us, is there some way I can say "Thanks!" in a clear, easily understood, and practical way? This part of the book's reflections describes how. Part 3 assumes that a thankful response to God's love will involve both active and contemplative, or prayerful, living. Such is human living at its best.

If our world needs anything today, it needs contemplatives-in-action. Much of what is wrong in today's world is because, as Isaiah said over two thousand years ago, too few of us think with our heart. We need people who pray or reflect over what makes us who we are when we are at our best. Not enough people reflect over God's constant care and guidance, God's self-revelation in myriad ways, and God's invitation to work with Jesus.

The ten reflections in this part of the book attempt to help us ask and tentatively answer: "Okay, how do I follow Jesus? How do I think with my heart and act from my true self, the way God sees me?"

Reflection 21

Come and Rest

Presence. Sit quietly. Ask to live more consciously in the presence of God.

Focus. Pay attention to your breathing. Gently release any thoughts that come to you, as they come to you. Keep returning to that place of quiet within, where God dwells.

Come and Rest

The apostles gathered around Jesus, and told him all that they had done and taught. He said to them, "Come away to a deserted place all by yourselves and rest a while." (Mark 6:30–31)

Comment

If our spiritual journey is anything, it is a story of God's communication and God's show of love for us, and the story of our responses. The next ten reflections are a chance to pause on life's journey to talk with Jesus about God's reaching out to you, and about your personal responses to the God who is love. Are we willing to pause and rest for a while?

For prayer over the next ten meditations, try to create a special spot in which to reflect and pray. Or enter imaginatively into the warmth and seclusion of Jesus' ever present embrace, there to be alone with him as your retreat master.

Openings for Prayer

Talk with Jesus, starting with these questions: Where am I on the journey of life? And where am I on my journey with you? Where would I like to be?

Do you have a specific resolve about retreats, prayer, or the way you follow Jesus as friend and coworker that you might want to consider during the next nine meditations?

Spiritual writer Leon Bloy claimed that the only real tragedy was not to become a saint. What do you feel about this?

Group Reflection and Sharing

What does the Scripture passage suggest about following Jesus?

How can a person "rest a while" with a job, family obligations, social commitments, and so on? What practical ways have you found? Do some brainstorming. Remember that even a few moments of rest can help.

What is your experience of retreats?

Many if not most people believe that the pace of life is too fast. Many would like to slow it down so as to have more time to savor the inward spiritual journey. Do you think it is time to promote this idea more strongly in your own life, in your family, among your friends, throughout American culture? Why? Will anyone listen?

Does this meditation suggest an idea for action?

Closing. Repeat the opening exercise of quiet attention to God.

Offer any intentions that come from your heart.

Prayer

Yahweh, my heart has no false pride;
my eyes do not look too high.
I am not concerned with great affairs
or things far above me.
It is enough for me to keep my soul still and quiet
like a child in its mother's arms.

(Psalm 131:1–2)

Reflection 22

Follow Me?

Presence. Try to recall how God is pleased with and attentive to your efforts to pray.

Focus. What, in your opinion, are some of the biggest barriers to following Jesus?

Follow Me?

[Jesus] said . . . , "Follow me." (Matthew 9:9)

Comment

The call to follow Jesus applies to us as well as to Jesus' Apostles. However, to do so, we will need to come to terms with two matters. First, God put us into existence without asking! And second, we are this or that kind of person and no other, and we are in these or those circumstances and no other. So, are we satisfied that God put us into existence? And are we at peace with ourselves, and do we accept ourselves as we are, and people, life, and God as they are? Note, "accept" does not necessarily mean that we are happy with everything. It simply means that we are willing to work with ourselves and with things as they are, even though we might wish that they were different.

Openings for Prayer

It is Good News to know that we are here for some good reason, so that right where we are and the very kind of person we are can be testaments to God's glory. Christ can live on in us and show his love. And we can become a better "us" here than anywhere else. For this, Jesus invites us to follow him. Pray over this for a while. Stay with it.

Jesus reassures those whom he had invited to follow him that "even the hairs of your head are all counted. So do not be afraid" (Matthew 10:30–31). He clearly wanted them to know that if they followed him, they would never be alone. Pray over these matters as you feel moved, and for as long or as short a time as you need to.

Group Reflection and Sharing

When you read the Scripture passage, what comes to mind? What does it suggest about following Jesus?

If you want to simplify your life, you could center it around one idea: When making choices, simply try to make those that would please Jesus and help him to live on through you. Can you see why acceptance of who you are is necessary for this?

What do you like best about the fact that you exist? What do you like best about your call to follow Jesus?

What things about life are hardest to accept? What can you do about them, or is a change of attitude the best solution?

What is most difficult about being called to follow Jesus?

Reflect on and then complete this statement: I may have my faults and limitations, but I like myself anyway because . . .

Does this meditation suggest some practical change you would like to make about following Jesus?

Closing. Reflect on some aspect of your life where you need to work willingly with things as they are.

Offer any intentions that are in your heart.

Prayer. Our gracious God, you created all things in wisdom and love that they may show forth your goodness and find their fulfillment in you. Help us to love ourselves rightly, even as you do. Free us to follow Jesus, so that we, too, may find you in all the events and circumstances of life. Glory to you, Source of all life, Word made flesh, and Spirit who lives within us, now and forever. Amen.

Reflection 23

Put Out into the Deep Water

Presence. Try to put yourself gladly and consciously into God's loving presence.

Focus. Recall an incident from *Rescue 911* or a similar story in which people responded to urgent human needs. Imagine a world in which people's service to one another on a daily basis was more important than self-centered concerns about getting ahead.

Put Out into the Deep Water

[Jesus] sat down and taught the crowds from the boat. When he had finished speaking, he said to Simon, "Put out into the deep water and let down your nets for a catch." Simon answered, "Master, we have worked all night long but have caught nothing. Yet if you say so, I will let down the nets." When they had done this, they caught so many fish that their nets were beginning to break. . . . When Simon Peter saw it, he fell down at Jesus' knees, saying, "Go away from me, Lord, for I am a sinful man!" . . . Then Jesus said to Simon, "Do not be afraid; from now on you will be catching people." When they had brought their boats to shore, they left everything and followed him. (Luke 5:3–11)

Comment

Following Jesus has the marvelous effect of helping us stop "sitting on our hands" and getting us into more generous whole-souled living. We become interested in and in love with God, in building the Reign of God, or in aiding people in need instead of focusing all our attention on ourselves. This is eminently healthy, good for relationships and for the whole of society. Sinful though we are, Jesus again tells us not to be afraid, even of the deep water.

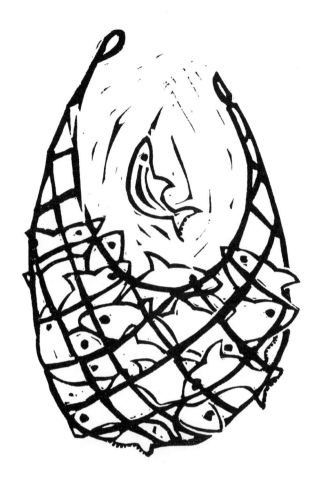

Openings for Prayer

Reread the passage from Luke quietly, slowly. Would you say about yourself what Peter said about himself? When Jesus tells you not to be afraid, what fears would he want to console you about? What deep water are you afraid of?

How are you going to "catch people"? As a follower of Jesus, what unique way of "fishing" do you have?

Group Reflection and Sharing

What does the Scripture passage suggest to you about following Jesus?

By deciding to try to follow Jesus, we can get on with life just as we do by losing ourselves in following him and by not worrying much about some deficiencies. Does this seem too simple? Is it hard to be this way?

What blessings from the society, country, neighborhood, or family make following Jesus easier? How can we take full advantage of such blessings?

It is obvious, too, that some things hinder us. What are the worst of those things? Is there anything we can do?

Anyone trying to follow Jesus likely feels torn between the ideal and the real. But isn't this tension okay? In fact it is a characteristic of an excellent Christian life! Reactions?

Closing. Focus on some specific step you want to take in order to follow Jesus more closely.

Offer any intentions that are in your heart.

Prayer. Jesus, you call us forth gently and firmly from our small world of self-concern. You invite us to a broader world of relationships, commitments, and unselfish love. Remove the fear that binds us and show us the path we must travel to follow you and share your work in this world. Amen.

Reflection 24

Following Jesus by Acts of Healing Kindness

Presence. With love in your heart, ask Jesus to let you know or feel his nearness.

Focus. Recall a time when your life was made a bit easier by someone's random act of kindness.

Following Jesus by Healing Kindness

Wherever [Jesus] went, into villages or cities or farms, they laid the sick in the marketplaces, and begged him that they might touch even the fringe of his cloak; and all who touched it were healed. (Mark 6:56)

Comment

A practical way to love Jesus in everyday life is by being a friendly, kind, and helpful presence to those close at hand. We are the healing touch of Jesus.

Jesus held all his sisters and brothers created in God's image as sacred. When we interact with anyone, we are interacting with the presence of Christ in our time. To see Jesus Christ in others is a matter of seeing them with faith, hope, and love as God's children, and as sisters and brothers in Christ, regardless of how they think, look, or act. We are simply trying to see what God sees.

Openings for Prayer

Are you content with the way you relate to people? Look at your past: Whom have you loved and hurt? And whom have you been loved and hurt by? Do you see any patterns or trends that would help you learn something about your best ways to be a friend who is trying to love and see Jesus in others? Or about things to avoid?

Why not begin the practice of kindness now? Choose the people to whom you want to relate better. Ask Jesus' help. Then plan the details and begin. Think of life as the opportunity for one-moment ministries, like greeting people with a smile and by name, showing simple courtesies like saying "Thanks," listening to people. Observe, as a side benefit, whether you feel unusually good as a result of your kindness.

Group Reflection and Sharing

What does this Scripture passage suggest about following Jesus?

People who are kind, understanding, patient, and gentle warm the heart. And pastors and parishioners appreciate few things more than a warm, friendly spirit in their communities. Can we keep this spirit even when dealing with irritating or aggressive people, especially with those whose opinions differ from ours?

Some commentators say that people are becoming increasingly brusque, dismissive, discourteous, aggressive, and even violent. Do you think this is happening? If so, how can we grow to be a kinder, gentler people? Or do the good and the gentle have to finish last?

Can you make kindness and friendliness personal with some idea for action?

Closing. With a grateful heart, pray for those who have gifted you with kindness: . . . (As each name is presented, all pray, "Kind God, bless those who bless us.")

With an open heart, pray for those who need kindness: . . . (As each person or group is mentioned, all pray, "Holy Friend, let us show your kindness.")

Prayer. Gracious God, we thank and praise you for your faithful love. Lead us beyond our self-centered concerns that we may be your healing presence for all in need. In Jesus' name we pray. Amen.

Prayer help. We can decide to grow in kindness, given God's abundant grace. Here are some points to ponder to help us grow in kindness toward others:

- Decide whom you think Jesus would like you to relate to better or be more helpful to among those with whom you work, play, or live.
- Begin by thinking of their best points, how Jesus loves them unconditionally, and how you would like to love them, too.
- Focus on one person at a time, in one particular difficult situation. Visualize the situation and person as clearly as possible, with details, colors, shapes, cast of face. Hear the tone of voice, initial greetings, and so on. Keep remembering that Jesus loves them. This might involve considerable compassion, recalling that to know all is to forgive all.
- Try to imagine exactly what Jesus would do in this situation. Try to think and even to feel as you think he might think and feel.
- Mentally go through your own situation in company with Jesus. See yourself, with his help, handling it exactly as he might, and trying to feel as he might.
- Give thanks to God that you are trying and that you are likely reacting better than you formerly did in this same situation. Thus you are readying yourself to put more of Jesus and love into the world when the situation actually arises again.
- If you can find something to like about the other person, dwell on this as much as possible.
- Keep your sense of humor about the situation!
- Keep praying and trying.

Reflection 25

Following Jesus by Praying

Presence. Always begin prayer by becoming calm and recalling God's presence.

Focus. What kind of time commitment is necessary to develop a significant relationship?

Following Jesus by Praying

[Jesus] was praying in a certain place. (Luke 11:1)

Comment

Like every devout Jew, Jesus probably recited the *Shema*, "Hear, O Israel . . . ," morning and evening. He also likely prayed the Eighteen Benedictions, morning and night. But Jesus also took time for prayer alone in deserted places, to be with God in an informal, personal way. Sooner or later, as with any friend, to develop and maintain a closeness to Jesus, we will want to spend time alone in his company.

A balanced prayer life would include meditating, communal worshiping, spiritual reading, an occasional examination of conscience, and watching for God in all things.

Openings for Prayer

Consider how to incorporate these five prayer practices—meditating, communal worshiping, spiritual reading, examination of conscience, and finding God in all things—into your life somehow. Ask Jesus what would be best for you at this time. You may not be able to manage all the practices at once. Try to be very specific as to when, where, and with what aids you will begin your prayer. Start small and expand as you feel moved. Confer with someone wise in the ways of prayer to help you find what suits you best.

To assist your reflection, look over the past: What have been your finest prayer moments? What have been your biggest neglects? What can you learn from these?

Group Reflection and Sharing

What does the Scripture passage suggest about following Jesus?

For a balanced life of prayer, how much time would a person need for each type of prayer: meditating, communal worshiping, spiritual reading, examination of conscience, and finding God in all things?

Each person's balance in prayer will be different. Some very busy people may have to confine themselves almost exclusively to finding God on the run! Why is uniqueness in prayer right and proper?

What has been your experience with these five prayer practices?

What place ought formal prayer enjoy in Christian life: for instance, prayers before and after meals, morning and evening prayers, prayers during Bible sharing, and so on?

A direct and meaningful form of meditation for many beginners is sacred reading. This means slow, thoughtful reading of the Bible or a good book, pausing wherever you find something of worth, and then talking with Jesus about what you found.

Closing. What commitment will you make to develop your relationship with God in prayer?

Offer any intentions that are in your heart.

Prayer

Jesus, like your disciples of old, we ask you, teach us to pray.
When our heart is full of joy and wonder, teach us to pray.
When we are weary and life seems too much, teach us to pray.
When we do not know how to pray, teach us to pray.
At all times, teach us to pray. Amen.

Prayer help. Daily companionship with God could begin in the morning with a moment to preview the day and ask for help. You could also conclude the day with a brief examination of how you found God in that day and by planning for tomorrow. This alone would be a good start to the spiritual life.

Reflection 26

Following Jesus by Reaching Out

Presence. Think for a moment about how God smiles on your efforts to pray and to serve people in need.

Focus. Look through the daily paper with an eye to people's needs for practical help, for compassion, and for justice.

Following Jesus by Reaching Out

"When [Christ] comes in his glory . . . he will separate people one from another as a shepherd separates the sheep from the goats. . . . [Christ] will say to those at his right hand, 'Come, you that are blessed . . . for I was hungry and you gave me food, I was thirsty and you gave me something to drink, I was a stranger and you welcomed me, I was naked and you gave me clothing, I was sick and you took care of me, I was in prison and you visited me.' Then the righteous will answer him, 'Lord, when was it that we saw you hungry and gave you food, or thirsty and gave you something to drink? And when was it that we saw you a stranger and welcomed you, or naked and gave you clothing? And when was it that we saw you sick or in prison and visited you?' And [Christ] will answer them, 'Truly I tell you, just as you did it to one of the least of these who are members of my family, you did it to me.'" (Matthew 25:31–46)

Comment

The Christian Testament is replete with stories about Jesus caring for poor and outcast people. He also criticized the institutions that were burdening them. Jesus commissioned his followers to carry on his concern. We are that group! And our task today is to help not only the poor individuals in local situations, but also to reach the institutions of society that perpetuate the plight of the underprivileged.

What the story of the Last Judgment suggests to Jesus' followers is first to get informed; then to talk, write, read, affirm, protest, contribute, speak, pray, phone, volunteer, take direct action—do whatever one can do to help people live with dignity. For some persons, the best beginning might be in their own backyard, although our backyard now seems to extend to the whole world.

Openings for Prayer

Sometimes the best way to get practical about anything is to say, after reconnoitering one's opportunities, "Jesus, where shall I begin?" Taking on only one issue is best for most people. Talk with Jesus about what your issue might be.

Can you think of some ways a prayerful person would look at reaching out to poor and outcast people? One way would be to think of Jesus suffering today in his mystical body and crying for help.

Group Reflection and Sharing

What does the Scripture passage suggest about following Jesus?

Have you noticed the pronounced interest in social justice by recent popes and bishops? What do you make of this?

What has been your experience of trying to foster social justice for needy people?

Do you feel sometimes that when it comes to making a better world, you are doing mostly maintenance? This may be all that is possible for you right now. If you feel overwhelmed by the difficulty of trying to make a difference for poor people, remember that the journey of a thousand miles begins with the first step. Also, Jesus does not ask for great results. He simply asks that we be faithful to our call, which is to include working for social justice in our practice of love of our neighbor, as well as in our concern for individual needs.

Does your community have a human rights or social-justice problem that could use attention?

Some positive actions for social justice would be to become informed and to raise questions in conversation. Then watch for an opportunity to get involved in an issue for which you feel special interest or compassion. Does this meditation suggest an idea for action?

Closing. Recall again the people of our world and their needs. Offer the petitions that come from your heart.

Prayer. Loving Creator God, we bring you our concerns for our brothers and sisters. (Take turns naming these concerns, responding, "God, help us to care for one another.")

[When your petitions are done, continue:] Our God, you are full of kindness and compassion for all your creatures. Enlighten our mind and encourage our heart as we strive to make your love known on earth. This we ask in Jesus' name. Amen.

Reflection 27

Following Jesus by the "Little Way"

Presence. Re-collect yourself. Prepare yourself to seek God's will during this prayer period. Ask that you may be generous, trusting, and willing.

Focus. Recall a significant practical decision that you have faced recently.

Following Jesus by the "Little Way"

I have come down from heaven, not to do my own will, but the will of [God] who sent me. (John 6:38)

Comment

Jesus' rule of life was to do the divine will for the sake of God's Reign. We know God's will for the big picture: to love God and our neighbor as ourself. The details are up to us to discern day by day, decision by decision. Catherine McAuley, founder of the Sisters of Mercy, said that holiness consists "in performing extraordinarily well the ordinary actions of every day. . . . 'Each action,' to use the words of a devout author, 'is all full of God, breathes of God, shines with God'" (*Familiar Instructions of Rev. Mother McAuley*, pp. 88–89). Thérèse of Lisieux called this the Little Way.

Even when it is difficult to know what to do tomorrow, it is usually clear what needs to be done today. Doing that, and doing it well and lovingly, is the best preparation for tomorrow. Keeping our attention to the task at hand is enhanced by prayer that keeps us centered on the loving God and God's priorities.

Openings for Prayer

Have a long talk with Christ about his will, and try to open yourself to some definite conclusion.

Today, ask God's guidance to do the ordinary tasks extraordinarily well. If you are washing dishes, just wash dishes. If you are talking with a friend or family member, be present, pay attention, just talk with them. Try to be present wherever you are and with whomever you are. At the end of the day, ask yourself, "How would it be to live this way?"

Group Reflection and Sharing

What does the Scripture passage suggest about following Jesus?

What has been your experience of hunting for what God wants of you?

Ignatius of Loyola outlined ways of discerning God's will and making Christian choices. His questions still provide useful direction for discerning God's will. Apply these questions, paraphrased from his *Spiritual Exercises,* to an issue that faces you or your community:
- If I were to advise someone I had never met on how a Christian would act in this case, what would I tell him or her to do?
- If I were on my deathbed looking back at my life, what would I have wanted to do in this instance?
- If I were standing before Christ at the Last Judgment and he asked about this decision, what would I want to be able to tell him?
- If I were advising someone I love in this matter, what would I tell her or him?

(Tetlow, pp. 60–61)

Review Catherine McAuley's statement about holiness consisting of doing ordinary things extraordinarily well—with love, attention, and faithfulness. How does this holy woman's advice match your concept of holiness? Does this sound challenging or too easy?

When making a difficult choice, have you found something that helps?

Considering the scope of Christ's teachings, what would constitute a list of the essential responsibilities for Christians?

Does the Little Way offer any wisdom to our culture's capitalistic and competitive spirit?

Does this meditation suggest anything practical for your everyday life? For instance, what about making a "morning offering" each day as a prayer to seek God's will?

Closing. Go back to the decision you recalled at the beginning of the meditation. Do you have a different frame for making the decision? any different feelings about your choice? additional options?

Offer any intentions that come from your heart.

Prayer

Happy are they whose way is blameless,
who walk according to your law.
Happy are they who observe your decrees,
who seek you with all their hearts.
They do nothing wrong
and walk in your ways.
You have commanded that your precepts
be faithfully obeyed.
I want to be firm
in keeping your statutes!

(Psalm 119:1–5)

Reflection 28

I Am the Vine

Presence. Recall God's indwelling presence and try to grow calm and be glad that your Creator is near.

Focus. When was the last time someone called on you for help? "Help" might involve time, resources, or simply listening. How did you respond?

I Am the Vine

"I am the vine, you are the branches." (John 15:5)

Comment

Jesus' declaration "I am the vine, you are the branches" makes it clear that he saw our relationship with him as intimate and interdependent. We gather our strength and foundation from him, and we grow inextricably connected with him. But the leaves on the branches serve the vine, too. Indeed, a vine stripped of its leaves and branches yields no fruit, withers, and dies.

Openings for Prayer

Ask Jesus about what sort of branch you are? What are the fruits of your branches? What is the harvest like?

Try to become fully convinced—Christ really wants you for a friend and also a coworker. Dwell on this until it sings in your heart. Can you see this fact as advantageous for you and for Jesus' work?

Try to envision, in all possible detail, the immense good to other people that will result from your life if you live closely with Christ, and how others may be influenced to follow him, too. Then, in prayer, let your feelings about this pour out to Christ.

Group Reflection and Sharing

What does the Scripture passage suggest about our relationship with Jesus?

If you ask yourself, Why follow Jesus? what are your strongest motivations? Compose a list and notice which reasons or feelings seem to occur most often. What do you make of your motivation?

Following Jesus is sometimes described as turning ourselves over to Jesus, deciding to live for him. How would you describe what it means to be as connected to Jesus as a branch is to a vine?

What problems can come with trying to follow Jesus?

How are my brothers and sisters helped by my living a Christian life both exteriorly and interiorly?

Do you think that Christ might be asking something of those in more affluent societies?

Closing. Spend a few minutes in silent reflection, filling in the blanks below. (A group member may then read each line, and participants who wish to may speak aloud a word or a phrase in response.)
- Jesus, at this time I think you may be calling me to . . .
- As I reflect on this call, I feel . . .
- I trust you because in the past you have . . .
- I ask you now for . . .

And we can offer other intentions that are in our heart: . . .

Prayer. Jesus, you call ordinary people, including ourselves, to be your disciples. You invite us to live your life and to be fruitful by carrying on your work in the world. You are always with us; help us to know that. Enlighten, strengthen, and console us as we grow in response to your love and your call.

> Use me, God, in Thy great harvest field,
> Which stretcheth far and wide like a wide sea;
> The gatherers are so few; I fear the precious yield
> Will suffer loss. Oh, find a place for me!
> A place where best the strength I have will tell:
> It may be one the older toilers shun;
> Be it a wide or narrow place, 'tis well
> So that the work it holds be only done.
> Amen.
>
> (Christina Rossetti, "Send Me")

Reflection 29

That They May Have Life

Presence. Place yourself in God's presence. Ask that you may be generous in following Jesus.

Focus. What value or values have the biggest influence on your choice of a job or ministry?

That They May Have Life

"I came that they may have life, and have it abundantly." (John 10:10)

Comment

Much has been made about Jesus' death on the cross. In fact, people emphasize it so much that they seem to forget that the Resurrection is actually the key event in the salvation of the world. Jesus brought life to the world; the Resurrection fulfilled his promise. Jesus teaches us how to live abundantly so that death need not be tragic. With faith, it becomes glory!

Openings to Prayer

As reasons for following or giving yourself to Jesus, which of the following have the strongest attraction? Ponder why you feel as you do.

Fulfillment. Jesus will assist me both by his Spirit and by his personal example to live and act lovingly.

Meaningful work. Since the world began, helping Christ establish the Reign of God is the work that matters most.

Enriched relationships. How can the kindness, prayer, and faithful love that come with following Jesus do anything but enrich all human relationships?

Enthusiasm amid boredom. One can now get enthused over any honorable occupation because, with a loving heart, one can do it for Christ.

Guidance for decisions. "What would Jesus like?" focuses all of my discernment.

Solace for the hurts of life. In Jesus, I have someone to live for in spite of the hurts.

Freedom. Jesus brings possibilities for new personal freedom from sin, death, and the Law; from having to be loved, esteemed, or to keep up with anyone; or from fear of dying with a meaningless life.

A sense of personal value. I am loved unconditionally. Because I am living for Jesus, I am always a worthwhile person, spending my time in worthwhile ways, which leads to an old age without regrets.

A friend. Jesus brings me himself as a friend, coworker, servant, a way in the dark, a song to my soul.

A model. Jesus is caring, loving, strong, principled, faithful, chaste, understanding—a wonderful mix of qualities.

Completion. Life in Jesus leads to happiness in this life and eternal reward in the next.

Hope for a better world. The more closely that people follow Jesus, including their action for poor and marginalized people, the better the world will be.

Are there any others that appeal to you?

Group Reflection and Sharing

Which of the previous reasons for following Jesus seem to mean the most?

Why might some people put off following Jesus? Is it good to approach people about this matter?

Do TV preachers give the right presentation about Jesus and how to follow him?

Does the church preach enough about Jesus?

If you were Saint Paul, what approach would you take when speaking about Jesus to today's world?

Some people are strongly attracted to a personal following of Jesus; others are not. Their spirituality may revolve around God, their neighbor, or virtuous living. The ways of spirituality are many. Do you have any comments about this?

No one can reincarnate Jesus totally. Francis of Assisi specialized in Jesus' poverty. Clare of Assisi exemplified Jesus' intimate union with God in prayer. Your call is to seek your special way, the way that is you at your best. What do you think it may be?

Does this meditation suggest something practical for action?

Closing. Reflect on this statement: "I best express Jesus in the world when I . . ."

Offer any intentions that spring from your heart.

Prayer

Lord my God, when your love spilled over into creation,
you thought of me. I am from love, of love, for love.
Let my heart, O God, always recognize, cherish,
and enjoy your goodness in all of creation.
Direct all that is me toward your praise.
Teach me reverence for every person, all things.
Energize me in your service.
Lord God, may nothing ever distract me from your love. . . .
neither health nor sickness, wealth nor poverty,
honor nor dishonor, long life nor short life.
May I never seek nor choose to be other than you intend or
    wish.
(Adapted from Bergan and Schwan, *Freedom*, p. 12)

Reflection 30

I Chose You

Presence. Remember God's presence as love by repeating silently the sacred name of God, "Love, Love . . ."

Focus. Ask God to remind you of a time when you were deeply aware of God's love for you.

I Chose You

"You did not choose me but I chose you." (John 15:16)

Comment

A worthy reason to follow Jesus is wanting to walk with Jesus because he has walked with me. I have been loved, gifted, forgiven my sins and failings, and called. The best response is a grateful heart coupled with a loving life.

Openings for Prayer

Take time. Review the notion of giving yourself to Jesus Christ through compassion, prayer, reaching out, and the Little Way.

If your heart is ready, compose some ritual or ceremony in which you offer yourself to Christ.

Meditate on this prayer of self-offering by Ignatius of Loyola:

> Take, Lord, and receive all my liberty, my memory, my understanding, and my entire will, all that I have and possess. You have given all to me. To you, Lord, I return it. All is yours. Dispose of it wholly according to your will. Give me your love and your grace. That is enough for me. (Tetlow, trans., *Spiritual Exercises of Saint Ignatius Loyola*, p. 79)

Group Reflection and Sharing

What did the Scripture passage suggest about following Jesus?

What predominant impressions have you gathered from this series of meditations?

Do you think your life will be any different from having made these reflections? in what ways?

Might you wish to do something as a group to follow up these meetings?

Closing. Design a short closing for this series and conclude with prayer together.

Prayer. End with the prayer of self-offering from the meditation.

Final Reflections

The foundation for a contemplative-active life is to live compassionately, to pray, to reach out in service, and to follow the Little Way of doing God's will. A developing awareness of God's constant, loving presence is an indispensable support for this contemplative-active life.

A contemplative-active person pays attention to how God is part of everything. The following prayer-poem by John Bowen reflects this contemplative-active awareness:

> I have seen a mother at a crib; so I know what love is.
> I have looked into the eyes of a child; so I know what faith is.
> I have seen a rainbow; so I know what beauty is.
> I have felt the pounding of the sea; so I know what power is.
> I have planted a tree; so I know what hope is.
> I have heard a wild bird sing; so I know what freedom is.
> I have seen a chrysalis burst into life; so I know what mystery is.
> I have fought and killed in a war; so I know what hell is.
> I have seen a star-decked sky; so I know what the infinite is.
> I have seen and felt all these things: so I know what God is!

Walt Whitman, in his nature poem "Miracles," found that almost everyone and everything he looked at seemed so full of wonder and complexity that it was a miracle.

> Why, who makes much of a miracle?
> As to me I know of nothing else but miracles,
> Whether I walk the streets of Manhattan,
> Or dart my sight over the roofs of houses toward the sky,
> Or wade with naked feet along the beach just in the edge of
> the water, . . .
>
> Every cubic inch of space is a miracle,
> Every square yard of the surface of the earth is spread with the
> same, . . .

To me the sea is a continual miracle,
The fishes that swim—the rocks—the motion of the waves—
the ships with men in them,
What stranger miracles are there?

To find God everywhere, we try to live more attentively and thoughtfully, and to put things in a spiritual perspective. We try to learn to look at things and react to them as God does or as Jesus does.

God's attributes are mirrored in nature, in people, in the universe, and they invite us simply to give praise. We find Christ and we can love, praise, thank, or petition him in everything and in everyone, in the worst as well as the best of times. Such is the way the saints lived. Such is the way we are all invited to live. Such is Christ's amazing grace.

Acknowledgments *(continued)*

The psalms in this book are from *Psalms Anew: In Inclusive Language*, compiled by Nancy Schreck and Maureen Leach (Winona, MN: Saint Mary's Press, 1986). Copyright © 1986 by Saint Mary's Press. All rights reserved.

The scriptural quotations cited as "adapted from" are freely adapted and are not to be interpreted or used as official translations of the Scriptures.

All other scriptural quotations in this book are from the New Revised Standard Version of the Bible. Copyright © 1989 by the Division of Christian Education of the National Council of the Churches of Christ in the United States of America. Used with permission. All rights reserved.

The excerpt on page 30 is from *Prayers for a Planetary Pilgrim*, by Edward Hays (Leavenworth, KS: Forest of Peace Publishing), page 97. Copyright © Forest of Peace Publishing, Inc., 251 Muncie Road, Leavenworth, KS 66048.

The excerpt on pages 31–32 is from *Come, South Wind*, edited by M. L. Shrady (New York: Pantheon Books, 1957), pages 151–152, originally published in *Ecclesia Orans*, edited by Dr. Ildefons Herwegen (Freiburg i.Br.: Herder and Company, 1937). Copyright © 1957 by Pantheon Books. Permission applied for.

The excerpt on page 96 is from *Familiar Instructions of Rev. Mother McAuley*, by Catherine McAuley (Saint Louis: Vincentian Press, 1927), pages 88–89. Copyright © 1927 by Vincentian Press.

The excerpts on pages 97 and 103 are from *The Spiritual Exercises of Saint Ignatius Loyola*, translated by Elisabeth Meier Tetlow (Lanham, MD: University Press of America, 1987), pages 60–61 and 79. Copyright © 1987 by the The College Theology Society, University Press of America. Permission applied for.

The poem on page 101, "Send Me," by Christina Rossetti, is taken from *The Treasury of Religious Verse*, compiled by Donald T. Kauffman (New York: Christian Herald Paperback Library, 1970), page 236. Copyright © 1962 by Fleming H. Revell Company. Permission applied for.

The prayer on page 104 is from *Freedom: A Guide for Prayer*, by Jacqueline Syrup Bergan and Marie Schwan (Winona, MN: Saint Mary's Press, 1988), page 12. Copyright © 1988 by Jacqueline Syrup Bergan and Marie Schwan, CSJ. Permission applied for.

The poem on pages 107–108, "Miracles," by Walt Whitman, is from *Leaves of Grass*, edited with an introduction by Sculley Bradley (New York: Holt, Rinehart and Winston, 1967), page 323. Introduction copyright © 1949 by Sculley Bradley.

KISSING
CALIGULA

Sam Harcombe

© Sam Harcombe 20

Acknowledgements

Thanks to *Poetry Monthly, Poetry Cornwall,
Purple Patch* and *The Journal,* in which
some of these poems first appeared.

Cover painting

The Great Leap by John Light

Printed by Poetry Monthly Press & Graphics
39 Cavendish Road, Long Eaton, Nottingham, NG10 4HY

Bumblebees

It's a good thing
no one told the bumblebees
they couldn't fly,
they might have believed it.

Aviation experts
made all the calculations
and announced that it was
mathematically impossible
for bumblebees to fly.

They were too heavy for their little wings,
non-aerodynamic,
power-weight ratio all wrong,
yet the bumblebees still flew.

Suppose someone does learn
their language and tells the bumblebees
to forget their wings and walk,
be sure they'll raise bee fingers
and keep on flying,
regardless.

Small Pools

Do fishes know
there's land out there?
Probably not:
they have enough to cope with.

Aren't we all
so much involved
with our own small pools,
that we have little idea
of others' needs
and motivations?

We watch them on the box,
but what do we know?
What do we understand?

Not much,
if we're honest.

Ultramarine

I'm ultramarine,
deep dark midnight blue,
the blue of the deeps of the sea.
Hear the west wind whistle
across the waves,
howl and roar round the rocks
and you hear me.

Ultramarine is wild, dangerous,
the colour of ocean deeps,
the depths of space.
Travel to these depths if you can,
swim in them if you dare,
you won't regret it;
but don't expect to stay the same.
No one visits my depths and is
unchanged, unmoved.
Who can say what the change will be,
but there will be change,
after you've been there,
seen the deep blue yonder.
heard the wind in the rigging,
felt your boat heel,
tasted the salt in the air,
the salt in your face.
Who knows what you will find in my sea deeps,
or in the ultra-far,
ultramarine depths of space.

There might be anything there,
anything at all.

Discovering Flight

What does the caterpillar imagine
as it pupates?
Does it know there's flying
and flowers to come
and sex?
As it lies in its chrysalis,
just surviving,
can it know what's in store?
Does it think it has already died?

What a wonderful moment
for that previously earthbound creature
when its wings dry out,
it spreads them
and flies away.

Guernica was the First

In any war civilians always suffer most,
ask the Trojans
or citizens of Armentières,
mustard gassed in 1918.

But at Guernica
destruction, death,
came suddenly,
unexpectedly,
from the air.
The German bombers
weren't even in a war,
just helping out their Fascist friends
and practising for 1939.
Was there a military target?
It's doubtful,
terror was their aim.
They knew they could do it
and wanted the World to see their power.
They destroyed,
killed,
terrorised,
and innocent civilians died.

Since Guernica it has always been the same;
Coventry, London, Bristol
Hamburg, Berlin, Dresden,
Tokyo.
Hiroshima and Nagasaki
were in a different class;
we pray there never is another such.
Even New York's been bombed.
All bombs kill the innocent;
TNT, napalm, nuclear, smart.
The last are supposed to destroy their target
and nothing else.
Anyone knows that's impossible.
There's always someone passing by,
and cleaners, cooks inside.
'Collateral damage' is the cold politician's term today
for slaughter of the innocents.

Who then are the terrorists?

Kissing Caligula

President Mitterand
said Margaret Thatcher
has the lips of Marilyn Monroe
and the eyes of Caligula.

What a terrifying thought:
to be made love to
while being assessed
for slaughter.

Life in Space

Is there life out there?
Somewhere in space
does one planet have microbes,
bacteria, viruses,
fruit flies?
They may not be sentient,
or humanoid,
little green men are hardly likely.

How many stars are there
in the sky?
No one knows for certain.
We do know
there are many galaxies,
all chock full of stars.
Each star's a sun
with planets circling round it
and most of those have moons
(Jupiter has at least sixteen).

Is it unthinkable
that one moon or planet
could have conditions possible for life?
Perhaps not breathing oxygen,
maybe not life as we know it,
but life?
In some form?

Don't tell me it's impossible,
you have no more chance of knowing
than I have.

Alert

The Chief Constable of Humberside
has had his car stolen.
His BMW with radio,
nee-naa siren
and blue flashers
is no longer where he left it.
The cop shops are empty,
no-one answers 999,
radio waves are jammed,
roads gridlocked,
panda cars are nose-to-tail
across the Humber Bridge
in both directions.
All the police are out
scouring Hull and Grimsby
for that car.

The CC's face is red
but not embarrassment,
it's rage.
They can hear his voice in Huddersfield;
he'll explode if his car's not found,
and quick.

Who stole it?
It's a special model,
highly desirable for export.
Would anyone deliberately
dare to liberate the Chief's own car?

More likely an opportunist thief,
saw his chance and seized it,
then discovered his mistake too late;
unless some crafty copper
had a grudge against his boss
and took this chance of getting back at him.

Whoever it was,
watch out.
Z Cars are after you,
the Bill is breathing down your neck
and Keystone Cops will catch you
if they can.

Based on a news item August 2002

I'm a Banana

ripe and ready for you.
Peel me
and I'll give you joy.
Bite me,
that's great for both of us.
Discard me
and I'll see you slip up.

Lucky Lightbulb

I expect you've noticed that metallic click
when a bulb goes as you switch it on.
No bang,
no flash,
just that little click...
then nothing.

I hope I go like that,
quickly, easily,
not long drawn out,
nor violently, disastrously,
'frightening the horses'
as Victorians put it.

Is the lightbulb lucky?
Not in the fact of going;
I've no more wish to be extinguished
than it has.
But if one day I go out with a click,
you'll know that was
just the way of going I hoped for.

Rememberings

If you can't remember the past
you may have to relive it.

There's a thought:
we all have heard
that history repeats itself,
and it's true.
Past wrongs, injustices,
might be forgiven,
hatchets buried,
peace established,
but forgiving
should not be followed by
forgetting.
The same person,
the same nation,
may not repeat the deed,
but the same pattern
will occur again,
and it is the pattern
we should remember
and watch out for.

based on a warning by George Santayana

A Sad Word

One of the saddest words of all
is a plain, simple,
mild expletive.

Black box recordings
reveal that before
nearly every air disaster
the last thing doomed pilots say,
in whatever language,
is just one word,

shit.

Sky Trail

Across the sky,
twin white stripes on blue.
Is it a fighter pilot
revelling in solo flight?
Or an airborne bus driver
bored by repetition,
held back by responsibility?

I stand in my garden,
earthbound,
and wishfully watch him pass.

A Closing

I grieved for my father:
his death was unexpected,
quick,
pneumonia with Alzheimers,
though that term
was unknown then.
There'd been disagreements;
I'd felt let down,
and allowed a coldness
to grow between us.

At his bedside,
in his final hours,
I held his hand,
he met my eyes
and smiled.
I think,
believe,
there was peace
and love
between us once again.

Now,
thirty years later,
I weep again for Dad.
I grieved
and still grieve
for the time we lost.
misunderstanding
misunderstood.
not trusting,
not talking.

Sleight of Mind

When a conjuror
plucks a coin from your nose
or a cardsharp
has all the aces,
quickness of the hand
deceives the eye.

If you ask a politician
an awkward question,
you often get the answer
to something else;
quickness of the tongue
misleads the ear.

If we catch a gambler cheating,
we don't pay up
or play with him again,
and if politicians evade our questions
we should insist on answers;
and maybe never fully trust them
in the future.
Quickness of mind
can perceive a slippery tongue.

Cerne Giant

Have you seen the Cerne Giant
as he strides across the Dorset Downs
swinging not just his club?
I wonder how many women
have worshipped him,
how many men have been inspired
to attempt excessive feats,
how many childless couples,
have conceived on that gigantic phallus.

Crablet

Attracted by warm autumn sea,
I remove my shoes and socks,
roll up my trousers and walk
along the tide's edge,
childishly paddling.
Sand grains collect
between my toes, washed
away by the next wave.
A tiny crab tries to dodge
my feet while doing his best
to bite me.
Scuttle off little crab, forget
about my toes, you're much
too small to nip them,
and I'll endeavour
not to trample you.

Whippet Walking

Taking three whippets for a walk
is not my idea of fun,
there's always one that goes
the wrong side
of any tree or lamppost.
Leads they tangle for a pastime,
wrap around my legs
and theirs.

Walking with three whippets,
they have all the fun.
If they see a cat
it's shout and shoulder-out-of-socket-time.
With other dogs reactions vary;
collies they detest,
barking, threatening,
ready all the time to run.

A whippet walking trio
gives scope for lots of fun;
The puppy tries to chase
any cyclist riding by
while the older dogs
look scornfully on.
Loose in woods, they're off like rockets
at first sighting of a squirrel.
Soon enough they're back,
their quarry up a tree.
Walking with three whippets
can sometimes be good fun.

Simple

"It's perfectly simple,
all you have to do is..."
An M.P. was talking
on the radio,
explaining how to deal
with some complex issue,
race relations,
crowded prisons,
public transport,
but as soon as I heard those words,
I switched off.

No matter how complicated,
how intractable
the problem is,
some silly ass thinks
he can sort it
at a stroke.
Even if there is an easy answer,
a way to cut
the Gordian Knot,
you can be sure that
anyone using that phrase
        is
    an idiot.

Based on a comment by Anne Fine
on Desert Island Discs.

19

What Next?

Is death so very final?
Is it our last resting place
or a junction,
a starting-off point
for a new existence?
No one knows.
I like to think
there is some sort of afterlife,
though Heaven or Hell,
perched on a cloud,
plucking at a harp,
or sitting on a griddle in a furnace
being jabbed with toasting forks
are too simplistic,
too puerile to consider.
Buddhists could be nearer
with their vision of a further life
in a creature higher or lower in the scale
according to the way we lived this life.

Bedbugs or plankton presumably
at the bottom
and mankind at top.
But why limit it to this small planet?
The Sun, our own star, has eight planets,
but up there in the sky
are millions or trillions of stars
and most of those have planets.
Why not a new existence as a bedbug
or some reasoning being on one of those?

Or could it be
that having sloughed off our human casing
we would be on a higher plane,
bodiless,
not tied down, constricted
by the finite,
but free
in the infinite?

Of one thing only am I certain.
There won't be harps or toasting forks.

Growing

With a reasonable degree of luck
we find that
growing old
is
unavoidable,
but many of us will
discover that
growing up
is
optional.

Other Means

War
has been described as
continuing politics
by other means.
Next time a
politician asks
for my vote
I'll make sure
he doesn't
pack a gun.

Wind Watcher

In the wind
the kestrel hovers,
twitching wings and tail
to stay in place,
keen raptor's eye
fixed on the ground,

ever watching.

Concerto

The first time I heard
Bach's Double Violin Concerto,
it was played by
David and Igor Oistrakh,
father and son,
separated by the Iron Curtain,
one in the West,
the other trapped in Russia,
their first meeting in twenty years.

The cascades of melody
their bows released
and the poignancy
of the occasion,
brought home to me
the evils of dividing countries,
splitting families.

Each time I hear the concerto
I remember the courage
and determination of
that father and son,
kept apart so long;
and I'm uplifted,
given hope.

Castration

For castration no knife is needed.
It's done every day
with acid words,
denigrating comments,
regular belittlement.
If a man, in Sainsbury's with his wife,
dutifully pushes the trolley,
picks up only what he's told
and is just an obedient helper,
he's castrated;
but if he chooses as he thinks fit,
whether right or wrong,
he regains his balls.

She's ready with her clippers
and will castrate you
if she gets the chance,
then when it's far too late,
regret it.
She doesn't really want a yes-man,
but a partner, a help-mate,
not a subservient slave.

So, hang on to your knackers,
lock up your bollocks.
It might seem she wants a eunuch,
who does just what he's told,
but she doesn't really.
So, next time you're told
exactly what to do, and how,
say 'Yes dear',
then go ahead and do it,
in your own sweet way.

Senses

To watch birds
in the ornithological sense.

To screw
in the engineering sense.

To know
but not in the biblical sense.

How disappointing!

Talking and Sleeping

men talk to women
so they'll sleep with them

women sleep with men
so they'll talk to them

perhaps if we all talked more
we would be happier

there might be more sleeping around
but would that be so bad?

Samson

Samson was strong;
he killed a thousand men
armed only
with a donkey's jawbone.
If that's difficult to believe,
try this:
his strength depended on his hair.
As long as it was uncut
he stayed strong.

Of course,
his downfall was a woman.
His ladylove, Delilah,
tricked his secret from him
and cut his curls off
while he slept,
then sold him to the Philistines.
He was blinded,
chained
and exhibited like a monkey
in the zoo.

Later,
tethered between two pillars
in the crowded temple,
he prayed for strength again
for just one moment.
His prayer granted,
he pulled down the temple
on the Philistines and himself.

The Bible doesn't say
what happened to Delilah.
She was well paid,
but did she suffer
from a guilty conscience?

Lonely Islands

We all have our own way
of being lonely.

We are individual,
and so is our loneliness.

We are islands to ourselves,
self-contained.

Donne was right,
we are all diminished
by others' losses,
their misfortunes,

but our loneliness
is ours alone.

Others can help assuage it,
to some extent,

but no one can share
our loneliness.

Love and War

Some say make love
not war,
some long for peace
not war.

Give me love
and peace any day,
but sometimes war is
unavoidable.

Let's just make sure it is
unavoidable
before deciding
on war.